Family
Expectations

Margaret Hill

ROSEN PUBLISHING GROUP, INC./NEW YORK

Published in 1990 by The Rosen Publishing Group, Inc.

29 East 21st Street, New York, NY 10010

Copyright 1990 by Margaret Hill

First Edition

Manufactured in the United States of America

Library of Congress Cataloging-in-Publication Data

Hill, Margaret
    Coping with family expectations / Margaret Hill—1st ed.
       p.   cm.
    Includes bibliographical references.
    Summary: Discusses family expectations of individuals, how they can be too harsh, too few, too mild, how they develop and affect the individual, and how they can be understood and handled.
    ISBN 0-8239-1159-4
    1. Expectation (Psychology)—Juvenile literature. 2. Teenagers—Family Relationships—Juvenile literature. [1. Expectation (Psychology) 2. Family life.] I. Title.
    BF323.E8H54   1990
    158′.24—dc20   90-30665
                                 CIP
             90-34018 AC

ABOUT THE AUTHOR ⋄

Margaret Hill has spent twenty years as a high school teacher and counselor in the areas of human behavior, creative writing, family living, child development, psychology, special education, and English.

She has been writing "practically forever": young adult novels, short stories, articles, poems, pamphlets, educational materials.

She took her BA in elementary education at Colorado State College of Education (now the University of Northern Colorado), and earned an MEd in Guidance and Counseling at the University of Wyoming, Laramie.

Her professional affiliations include membership in various associations representing mental health, mental retardation and other disabilities, education, guidance and counseling, writing, alcoholism and other drug dependencies, and retirement.

She and her husband, Bob Hill, are the parents of three daughters and one son, now married and away from home.

Contents

CHAPTER 1

Expectations
Begin at Birth

You don't remember what happened when you were born, but at that very moment of entering your new world something was expected of you. What was it, and by whom? You were expected to cry, and if you didn't, your audience—doctor, nurses, parents (perhaps)—became alarmed. Why? Because that first cry was a survival measure. It drew air into your lungs so that you could start breathing, and you are expected to go right on breathing until you die. Breathing is an *involuntary* function—one that we don't think about.

But breathing isn't all that is expected of you. For a lifetime you are surrounded by the expectations of your world; of your parents, caretakers, teachers, and others who are in a position to direct your life; of yourself (what do *I* expect of *me*?)

Sometimes we feel as if we are smothering in the "have-to's" and "ought-to's" of life, but those expectations are guides that help us grow into worthwhile and satisfied

1

human beings. At the same time they are the source of many problems. So let's look at what goes wrong when expectations are too harsh, too few or too mild, or not understood.

EXPECTATIONS CAN BE A PAIN

Expectations are fragile and ever-changing, depending on time, place, situation, and the people involved. They are based on needs. You expect something of someone, depending on one of your wants. Others expect things of you depending on their desires. Needs involve feelings, and because we often can't read one another's emotions, expectations can result in deep disappointment.

Let's see how an expectation can cause pain. Suppose you are an identical twin, age five. Your twin is playing on the porch when your dad comes home from work. You are in the living room. Dad greets your twin affectionately. Then he comes into the house, but before he sees you he stops in the front hall to look at the mail. There he finds a bill he has already paid. His good mood changes to one of annoyance. He goes through the living room muttering to himself in search of your mother to tell her about the bill mix-up. He doesn't notice you. Although he is the same father who came home a few minutes ago, your twin sees him as cheerful and loving, while you perceive him as angry and indifferent. This has a bruising effect on your ego; since you and your twin are alike, you expect to be treated that way. At age five, you aren't thinking about other people's frustrations. All you know is, you didn't expect to get a brush-off from your father.

That incident is only one small disappointment in the child's life, and it will soon be forgotten as long as the warm father-child relationship continues.

It is when expectations are severe and ongoing that personality damage occurs. But why can't we just ignore hurts and disappointments? It seems that we could simply say, "That's over; it has nothing to do with now." The trouble is, the past has lots to do with now.

MEMORIES ARE POWERFUL

Somewhere in your brain is a memory bank. Everything that happens to you is stored there, even though you can't consciously recall all of it. Some of those happenings that you can't remember can cause pain, unhappiness, fear, and even illness because some feeling or combination of feelings got buried along with the happening.

Members of a Family Living class talked about past incidents that stand in the way of getting on with life.

Marcie remembered a family crisis that occurred when she was six. "It was bad enough having my mother gone from home for several days, but when she came home with a brand-new baby, I was really upset."

"That should have been a nice thing," Trish commented.

After some discussion, the class agreed that a child's reaction to a new baby would depend on how the parents handled the situation.

"So in your case, Marcie, it was an unhappy event?" Miss Alvarez, the teacher, suggested.

Marcie said, "It started out that way. I'd been the attention-getter for six years, and now suddenly here was this homely, squirming kid. I couldn't figure out why everyone was making so much of him. No hair, no teeth. He didn't laugh or talk or play. It seemed to me he was always being fed or talked to or rocked. Then there were lots of visitors bringing presents and fussing over Jason."

"Didn't your parents prepare you for how things would be when the baby came?" Evelyn asked.

"They are the kind of parents who would have," Marcie explained, "but my mother was sick during the entire pregnancy and spent much of it in the hospital. My parents didn't talk with me about the baby because there was a good chance that Mother wouldn't be able to carry it to term. They didn't want me to be disappointed."

"So how did you handle the situation?" Miss Alvarez asked.

"I don't remember exactly. Sulked, probably. Acted up. I do remember purposely knocking my glass of milk over one evening. I expected my parents to bawl me out, but they didn't. I think they knew I was feeling hurt and left out. Later Dad took me on his lap and read to me. From then on, Mom let me help take care of the baby, which turned out to be fun. The best thing of all was that after a while Jason waved his arms and acted happy when he saw me."

Another student, Perry, remembered a day in second grade when he returned to school after being out sick. "There I was," he said, "standing behind some girl named Alice. We were waiting for the teacher to take our absence excuses. The teacher said, 'We missed you, Alice.' But when she took my excuse, she didn't say anything. I really felt cut down."

Because Perry expected, or at least hoped, to receive the same consideration as Alice, his self-esteem took a tumble. All of us have many episodes of that nature, but there are usually enough good ones to balance things out. That's what keeps us healthy and sane—getting knocked down and bouncing back up. But suppose you continually have bad experiences or fail over and over. Soon your self-concept may become so tattered that you no longer feel like an all-right human being. Your mind is packed with memories that hurt, and that can keep you from functioning satisfactorily.

EXPECTATIONS FASHION BEHAVIOR

Psychologists talk about "self-fulfilling prophecy." That means that we tend to live up to what others expect of us. Let's assume that Perry's classmate Alice was a good student, enthusiastic about school. Naturally, people expect her to be an achiever, and the more they approve her performance, the more motivated she is to fulfill their expectations.

Perry, on the other hand, has been babied a great deal and so tends to come across as childish. He hasn't experienced success in learning any particular skills, so he has no confidence that he could do anything as well as others his age. Because he fails more often than he succeeds, he expects to fall short, and others expect the same of him. Perry's name becomes associated in his own mind and in the minds of others with the word "loser," whereas the Alices are automatically thought of as "winners."

Like Marcie's experience, most incidents, whether remembered or forgotten, do not leave permanent scars. Life is made up of the woeful and the wonderful. Both have an influence on personality, but not necessarily a damaging one. What matters is the repeated pattern of fail/lose or of succeed/win.

Miss Alvarez's students asked what they could do about getting on a succeeding track with a background of defeating memories. "After all, the memories are already there," Perry pointed out. "We can't change them."

"Think about that for a few minutes," the teacher told the class.

Finally Roy said, "Do you mean what happens to us now will be a memory later on?"

Miss Alvarez nodded. "Exactly. Start packing fulfilling experiences and warm feelings on top of the painful ones."

Perry sighed. "If I only knew how!"

Miss Alvarez said, "We'll start with an assignment. Now, don't groan yet. This is something different. Today's actions are tomorrow's memories. Each of you is to create a memory this very day to store away for the future. Do or say something that will make you *and* another person feel good. Tomorrow we'll talk about it."

The students looked doubtful, but they were used to Miss Alvarez's offbeat assignments, and this was preferable to having to write something.

The next day several had rather enthusiastic reports:

"I helped Mom get supper. We got to visiting and talked to each other more than we have for a long time."

"Dad offered to help me build my 4-H booth for the carnival. I really wanted to do it myself, but I figured it would make him feel good if he thought I needed his help. I felt good, too, when I saw how pleased he was. We don't do things together very often."

"I decided not to annoy the study hall teacher for once. Instead I worked on my algebra and practically understood it for a change."

"I went to the senior center and gave the flower arrangement we made in art class to a lady who used to be our neighbor. She practically cried and kept holding my hand."

"Perry, did you carry out the assignment?" Miss Alvarez asked.

"I sure did. I took my kid brother to the carnival. He was so excited he couldn't eat supper, but he made up for it with popcorn and cotton candy."

Miss Alvarez laughed. "Not exactly a well-balanced

meal, but what you did for him was worth more than the supper he missed. Emotional needs are as important as physical ones. Judging from your reports, class, several of you brought a shaft of sunlight into someone's day. Did it do anything for your self-esteem?"

Most of the pupils admitted that making someone else feel better helped them to feel good about themselves.

Miss Alvarez said, "If you want to form the habit of being a worthwhile person and of having a satisfying life, live each day as if you were going to ask someone to write a recommendation letter for you describing your good qualities."

"What if you don't have any good qualities?" Perry asked.

"Perry, that's what this class is all about. Everyone has good qualities. Every day we need to be using those positive characteristics the way you did for the assignment. At the same time, we should look at ourselves honestly and decide what we don't like so we can get rid of those qualities."

"Like weeding a garden," Connie suggested.

"A good comparison," Miss Alvarez approved. "Kill the weeds and care for the flowers. And there's the bell. Remember, what you do with the rest of the day will be memories tomorrow."

PLEASANTLY UNEXPECTED; DISAPPOINTINGLY UNEXPECTED

Notice that the things the students did in response to the assignment were pleasant surprises because of not being expected by the other person. One of Miss Alvarez's assignments was to write a few paragraphs with the title, "It Wasn't What I Expected." Some of the situations described were disappointments that occurred when expectations were not fulfilled. Others were the surprised and pleased reactions to something that had not been expected. The most dramatic account was Jessica's. "I telephoned my dad last night," she said.

That announcement didn't get much reaction until Jessica explained that her father had deserted her and her mother when she, Jessica, was two years old. Since her marriage did not fulfill her expectations, and because she had suffered a rejection by a key person in her life, Jessica's mother had nothing good to say about her ex-husband. Furthermore, she expected Jessica to detest him also.

Class members decided that Jessica's mother was justified in hating the man and that it wouldn't be any wonder for Jessica to feel the same way. At that point, they were eager to hear why Jessica had called him the night before.

"A couple of years ago my father got in touch with us," Jessica told them. "Said he wanted to get acquainted with his daughter. You can imagine how upsetting that was to my mother, and what a shock it was to me. I had always been hurt because I didn't have a father like most kids. In fact, I kept expecting my mother to get married again. Even a stepfather would be better than none, I argued, but she wasn't about to get into another trap."

Jessica said that her father had called often after that, saying how sorry he was for the way he had treated his wife and child and wanted to make it up to them. "Dad actually expected Mom to take him back as if nothing had happened," Jessica said.

"What did you expect?" Miss Alvarez asked.

"I didn't imagine Mom would go along with that, but I wanted it to happen—that we would all be a family again. Mom refused to let me stay on the phone when he called, and she wouldn't let me answer letters and cards he sent on birthdays and holidays."

"How did you get up the nerve to call him last night?" Perry asked.

"I'm not sure," Jessica admitted. "I've been feeling so awful—as if I was being ripped apart by these two parents. Suddenly it didn't seem fair. Maybe I had a right to get to know this guy who is, after all, my own father. I wanted to say that to Mom, but I didn't dare. She was at a meeting yesterday evening, so I just decided to call the number Dad had sent on one of my cards. My conscience was giving me fits, but calling him still seemed like something I had the right to do."

"What would have happened if you had told your mother what you were going to do?" Miss Alvarez asked.

"I'm sure she would have laid down the law, and then I would have been going against her orders."

Jessica continued, "I half hoped he wouldn't answer the phone, and when he did my voice was so clogged up that I could hardly tell him who I was. When I finally did, he sounded so happy I thought he was going to cry. After we talked a while, I told Dad I would have to tell Mother I had called. For one thing, she would find out when the phone bill comes, but in any case I couldn't keep a secret like that without feeling guilty."

"Guilt is a difficult emotion to deal with," Miss Alvarez said. "I am glad you do feel guilty, because that means you have a conscience. Conscience is that parent inside of us that keeps us out of trouble if we listen to it."

Someone in the class suggested that Jessica might role play with a classmate to practice how she might tell her mother what had happened, and what she might do about the situation from then on. The outcome of the role-playing was Jessica's deciding that not only would she tell her mother about the phone call, but she would be assertive enough to say that she would be calling her dad again and writing to him.

Evelyn, the student who played Jessica's mother, said, "Look here, Jessica, I simply don't want you to get hurt. How can we know that this man has really changed?"

"We don't know," Jessica admitted, "but I'm willing to take that chance. Mom, you can't know how exciting it is to actually have a father who acts like a father. Seems to, anyway. And if it turns out that he lets us down again, I think I can handle that. After all, life isn't always the way we want it to be."

"You girls handled that interview very well," Miss Alvarez approved. "It may not go that smoothly when you actually face your mother, Jessica, but it seems to be something you have to do. The important thing is that you know it could end disappointingly, and you are prepared to face that. Right now your expectation is that whatever the outcome, it will be no worse than all those years without a father."

CHAPTER 2

I Should Have
Been a Boy!

Family expectations began even before you were born. Parents not only expect a child, they expect a certain kind of child—healthy, beautiful, and intelligent, probably. Sex preference often enters into it. The parents may have chosen only girls' names or boys' names, so sure were they that the child would be female or male. Nevertheless, the newcomer is usually welcomed with wonder and love regardless of sex.

Mrs. C. describes her anxiety during her fifth pregnancy. "We already had four girls," she explains. "Ben absolutely had his heart set on a boy this time. I was truly anxious about how he would accept the baby if it turned out to be a girl. I needn't have worried. You hear a lot about bonding between a mother and her newborn baby. In our case, the bonding appeared to be between Ben and little Carolyn the moment she was born."

Not all parents adjust to a birth disappointment the way Ben C. did. Have you ever had the suspicion that one or both of your parents sometimes wish you were the opposite sex?

In the case of Jake B.'s family, there has never been a question about Jake's preferences. Jake is a rancher from a family of seven sons. He is "a man's man," strong, virile, macho, and hard-working. He lives for his ranch and the outdoors. So determined was he to have sons that when each of his four daughters was born, he gave her a name that could belong to either a boy or a girl. What effect does this narrow attitude have on his children? Jake's daughters didn't mind being interviewed and written about. The names, including Jake's, have been changed for this account.

The oldest girl, Teddy, says she has no problem with Jake's wishing she were a boy. "He and I get along fine," she said. "My greatest satisfaction is being a rancher, and nowadays women can be anything they want to. Dad and I work right along together. He thinks of me as a man, and I think of me as a woman, but we both think of me as a rancher."

What about Jake's wife?

Teddy says that she is a loving, caring mother but a submissive wife. Her parents grew up in Sweden at a time when women were more domestic than they are now. Jake thinks of her as someone to cook and keep house and be a mother to his children. He is never cruel or brutal to his wife, but tends to be indifferent. This apparently doesn't bother Melva, who also thinks of women as belonging in the home.

What is Teddy's attitude toward men? She likes men and feels comfortable with them. She says she will probably marry someday, but for now she is so busy rounding up cattle, working in the hay field, and participating in rodeos that she hasn't time for romance. In answer to a question about her own sexuality, Teddy said, "I don't give it much thought. I like being a woman as long as I can do what I am doing, but I wouldn't mind being a man, either."

Jake's second daughter, Billie, married as soon as she graduated from high school and now has a daughter. She and her husband, Carl, own a motel in a small town in another state. "I didn't pay too much attention to Dad," she confided. "I spent a lot of time helping with the chores, but I also helped Mom with the housework. I didn't approve of her taking orders from Dad and waiting on him, but that was the way she was brought up, and I guess it's a good thing. Otherwise, there would have been fireworks between them! Dad got so much satisfaction from Teddy's turning out to be such a great rancher that he wasn't too disappointed in the rest of us. He did nag us a lot, though, about not working hard enough, and he was always gruff, never affectionate. I don't remember Dad's ever kissing us or holding us on his lap or anything like that."

Rae, the third-born of Jake's daughters, was the least eager to talk about her childhood. At the time of the interview she was a senior in high school. With her boy's attire and short hair, it was hard to tell whether she was boy or girl. Even her voice was neither decidedly masculine nor feminine, but a moderate in-between. With the current unisex trend in society, it isn't unusual for boys and girls to look alike. The disturbing thing about Rae was that she had not established her own sex identity.

When asked how she felt about being treated more like a boy than a girl by her father, she said, "I feel like a jigsaw puzzle piece in the wrong box. I have trouble thinking of myself as a girl; still, I don't feel like a boy, either. I'm sure Dad sees me as a boy, and to Mom I'm just one of her children. It's at school that I rattle around not quite belonging with any group. The guys don't want me hanging around with them the way I did when I was little. Then I was just thought of as a tomboy, but tomboys aren't *in* when you get to junior and senior high school. And I'm sure not someone the guys want to date. But I don't fit in any better with the girls."

In answer to a reminder that Teddy felt comfortable with both boys and girls, Rae said, "It's different with her. Teddy is glamorous—goes in for fancy cowboy boots and expensive Western clothes for women. She has been rodeo queen, and that's a status symbol in this community."

Rae says she has no homosexual tendencies—doesn't, in fact, have romantic feelings for members of either sex. "It's more a matter of not knowing who I am or what I am," she said in a wistful voice. "The other three seemed to be satisfied with who they were, even though Dad thought of us as boys. All except Toni, that is."

What was different about Toni, the youngest of Jake's daughters?

Her appearance, for one thing. Petite and fragile-looking; red hair, worn Afro style; green eye makeup; dressed in brightly colored shorts, a frilly white blouse, and green sandals; several pairs of earrings, and gold chains on wrists and ankles. Everything about Toni's looks added up to the word "girl." Even her voice was little-girlish, almost petulant.

How did Jake react to this daughter?

Toni laughed when asked that question. "By the time I came along, Dad was probably so disenchanted that he didn't give a hoot what I was. He had done a pretty good job of making believe the other kids were boys, so one huge disappointment didn't exactly ruin his life. Mostly he doesn't pay much attention to me. He found out early that he couldn't order me around the way he does the others.

Besides, I was no good at ranch work and outdoor chores. I'm not even crazy about horses."

How did the rest of the family see Toni?

According to her sisters, Toni was like a family pet. A real joy to her mother, willing to be inside helping with cooking and housework rather than outdoors with her father. A diversion for Teddy and Billie, who sometimes joined Toni in experimenting with makeup and novel hair styles. A family problem much of the time because of unwillingness to conform to rules about coming right home from school, getting good grades, observing curfews, not dating older men, and other expectations that the other girls took for granted.

Of Jake's four girls, each has chosen a role and adjusted to the family situation in her own way. All except Rae appear to be surviving in fairly normal fashion. Teddy, Billie, and Toni have decided who they are and are satisfied with their choices. Besides being Jake's daughters, they belong to themselves. Only Rae, at the time of being interviewed, had not established a sense of self-identity. She, perhaps, will need professional help in finding herself.

WHO IS THIS NEWCOMER TO THE WORLD?

Self-identity begins at birth when the person enters the world bringing with him or her a vast backlog of heredity, both physical and mental. From that moment on, everything that happens to the person has an impact on who he/she turns out to be. Life is a constant striving to maintain a balance between what is expected of you and what you expect of yourself. That depends on the way you see yourself and the way others perceive you. Your parents begin to build an image of you even before you are born.

When asked what they want for their children, parents invariably answer happiness. Another common response is success. As you grow and develop, you also probably think of success as a long-range goal. So where is the conflict between your expectations and those of your parents? Your idea of success may be different from theirs.

Seventeen-year-old Raymond decided that he didn't want to be in school, but he was afraid to tell his father. He could imagine how his parents would react to his dropping out of high school in junior year. After all, Dad was a college professor and had brought Raymond up with the idea that of course everyone goes to college. So Raymond chose a quiet way to get his message across: He simply quit attending classes. Every day Raymond's father drove him to school and watched him enter the building. Raymond then left by another door and spent the school hours out on the town. At the end of the day he would be waiting at the school to be picked up by his father.

This pattern didn't last long because school authorities notified Raymond's parents about his absence from classes. The scene between Raymond, his parents, and the school principal had its stormy moments. However, Raymond finally put into words his desire to move to another state to work for his brother and attend an automotive school in the evenings.

"Your mother and I never knew that you were interested in mechanics," Raymond's father said.

"I was afraid to tell you," Raymond said. "I figured you'd go through the ceiling."

"I probably would have," his father admitted, "but that would have been better than this truancy."

IT'S NOT WHAT YOU SAY, BUT HOW YOU SAY IT

Human behavior experts are in agreement that probably the greatest obstacle to satisfying relationships among people is communication. Why is it so difficult for us to convey what we want to say without hurting ourselves or others?

A major reason is anxiety about how the other person will react to our message, as in Raymond's situation.

Basically, there are three ways to "come across" to people—submissively, assertively, and aggressively. How do these differ? An example of submissiveness is the way Jake's wife, Melva, responded to her husband's wishes. Melva settled into her expected role of mother, wife, and housekeeper without argument. Jake's daughter Rae was submissive to Jake's perception of her as a boy. Unlike her sisters, Rae made no effort to assert feminine character-istics along with the expected masculine ones.

Jessica, the girl who decided to telephone the father who had deserted the family years before, used the word "assertive" in explaining her action. She said that she would be assertive enough to tell her mother that she would call her father again. Where is the line between assertiveness and aggressiveness?

An example might explain. Fifteen-year-old Lissa had been carrying around a load of anger for months, perhaps years, because she felt that her parents favored her brother, Rex. As a child, Lissa had a quick temper that often landed her in trouble. Gradually she had learned to control the temper, but at the same time she developed a pattern of covering up her feelings. She was considered an agreeable, easygoing child. Her behavior was usually submissive, but her feelings were not so mild.

One evening, after a trying day at school, Lissa was ordered to do homework while Rex was allowed to watch TV. Suddenly Lissa's anger erupted in a storm of profane accusations against Rex and her parents.

As usually happens during such a crisis, the family members displayed their ugliest behavior. Rex ran out of the house. Lissa's father slapped her—something he had never done before. Lissa's mother cried and became extremely upset. Lissa's stomach was a knot of pain, and she felt as if her whole safe world had fallen apart around her. Besides the physical pain and the emotional hurt, Lissa was overwhelmed with guilt at the effect of her outburst.

After a miserable, irrational night, the family was ready to discuss the situation somewhat calmly.

What had gotten into Lissa? her parents wanted to know.

She was tired of their favoring Rex, she informed them.

Why hadn't she said so? they demanded.

Because they wouldn't have listened, she told them.

"We're listening now," her father said.

That opened the way for all members of the family to express their feelings, to explain their behavior, and to admit their mistakes. They chose their words carefully and resolved several of their problems.

The way Lissa brought her problem out in the open was aggressive. The way she talked about it the next day was assertive.

Aggressiveness means expressing yourself in an intimidating, overpowering way without regard for the other person's feelings. As one teenager expressed it, aggressiveness is "running over people like a steamroller." *Assertiveness* means expressing what you consider to be your rights, your feelings, and your opinions, but doing so in the least hurtful way to yourself and others involved.

Assertiveness can also mean hurting someone temporarily to prevent greater pain in the long run. A common problem among teenagers is a reluctance to break off a relationship. Typical expressions of this are, "I can't bear to tell Clifford I've met a guy I like better than him." "I don't enjoy being with Sue Lynn any more, but she will be crushed if I break off our friendship." "I've decided I'm not ready to get married, but I don't have the nerve to tell Mary."

While it may be painful to voice such feelings, continuing a relationship that is no longer satisfying can only lead to deeper pain later.

Sometimes people really won't listen and the assertive method doesn't work. It may be necessary to bring about a crisis to let people know you are close to desperation. Before doing so, though, be sure you have tried to communicate your problem with words.

Aggressiveness does not necessarily mean blowing up or being loud and abusive. Aggression can be a quiet, undercover behavior designed to manipulate people. Psychologists refer to this type of behavior as "passive-aggressive." Although Raymond did not blow up at his parents, his undercover method of bringing them to his terms would be labeled "passive-aggressive" by behaviorists.

UNWANTED

Whether parental expectations are reasonable or unreasonable, they serve as guidelines. Expecting something of children means caring about them. The most unfortunate babies are those born to parents who didn't want them in the first place and didn't change their minds when the children were born. Those are babies born without expectations.

So much is said and written about how critical love and care are during birth and the early months of life that we may get the impression that the child born to uncaring, unfit parents is forever lost.

Students in Mr. Barkhurst's Psychology class talked about that. Richard's comment was, "We're always being told that a child's character is formed by age five, or maybe seven at the latest. That seems pretty final. It's like someone saying to the parents, 'This was your last chance and you blew it. Tough!'"

Mr. Barkhurst said, "Let's follow through on that. Suppose we have this imaginary child, Bobby. His parents didn't want him to begin with. His mother neglected her health during pregnancy. Bobby didn't receive love as an infant; therefore, he didn't learn to trust people at an age when trust develops. Bobby received no discipline other than physical brutality. Consequently, he developed some monstrous behaviors. His parents couldn't stand him, so they shipped him off to relatives. By age seven, Bobby keeps the second-grade class in a state of turmoil, and his teacher is headed for a nervous breakdown. As a result of seven years of poor nutrition, Bobby is frail and undersized, and his teeth are rotten. So is his personality, because he hasn't learned anything about the art of living."

"Wow!" Clayton exclaimed. "No one's that bad off."

"Believe me, it happens over and over," Mr. Barkhurst said. "So do we decide there's nothing anyone can do about Bobby? Shrug our shoulders and say, 'Sorry, little fellow, you turned out to be a mess through no fault of your own, but it's too late to do anything about it. Now go your destructive way, and eventually you'll wind up in prison or a mental hospital.'"

Richard said, "I see what you're saying. We shouldn't give up on a person."

"Exactly," the teacher agreed. "Suppose this same Bobby hadn't learned to add in the first grade. Would the second-grade teacher decide, 'Too bad. You'll never learn any more math as long as you live because you missed out on first-grade skills'?"

Lorene said, "A good teacher takes the student from where he or she is and teaches what the kid ought to know. I guess we have to do that with behavior, too."

Not only should you take others from where they are, but you owe that to yourself. You probably aren't totally happy with yourself. You wish you were different in at least some ways. What keeps you from becoming that great person you dream of being? Perhaps the largest block is the attitude, "That's just the way I am." Deciding that you are a certain way and nothing can be done about it is like casting your personality in concrete. Regardless of what happened to you at birth and what is expected of you now, you can take charge of your life and set up some expectations of your own.

CHAPTER ◇ 3

Ouch, My Need
Got Bumped!

Miss Alvarez greeted her class one Monday morning with the statement, "I have a question for you."

That got the students' attention, because this teacher's ideas were usually worth thinking about.

The question was, "Are you fed up with the news we are constantly bombarded with—the homicides, suicides, gang warfare, AIDS epidemic, the homeless, the battered, the alcohol-related incidents, the drug-addicted—" Miss Alvarez paused, and the students began to wake up from their Monday morning lethargy. They knew they were expected to come up with answers, and not just empty ones.

"I've gotten so I don't listen to that stuff," Linda said finally.

The teacher nodded. "You've just made the point I want to emphasize. You have quit listening to and reading the grim news because you expect it."

"Well, we have to expect it because that's how it is," Roy said.

Miss Alvarez said, "That makes my second point."

By now the students were looking uncomfortable, wishing they hadn't opened their mouths to make the teacher's points.

Her second point was, "You have decided that this is the way things are and there's nothing you can do about it. When people accept an ailing society, they give up on trying to make it well."

"We're tired of all those things you mentioned," Jessica said, "but we don't know what to do about it."

Miss Alvarez suggested, "Suppose everyone in the world were loving and caring. Those are two key words in human relationships—loving and caring. If everyone were that way, most of our social problems, including war, would disappear."

"But not all people are that way," Perry protested, "and they're never going to be."

"You're right about that," Miss Alvarez admitted. "But what if each of us in this room were more loving and caring than we are."

"Oh, oh, here comes the assignment," Richard said.

"You're right about that, too," the teacher said. "There has to be one single thing that each one of us in this room can do this very week toward mending the world."

"Like what?" Bart asked.

"Like what you say to someone, or how you say it. Suppose, for example, I were to zero in on one of you and say, 'You're doing a rotten job in this class. We'd be better off without you.'"

"You'd never say anything like that," Jessica protested.

"Suppose I did. How would you feel if you were that person?"

Right away the students' reactions began to tumble forth: "Hurt." "Furious." "Embarrassed." "Mad." "I'd hate you."

"So what would you do?" the teacher interrupted. "Start being a good student so I'd like you and give you a good grade?"

"No, I'd walk out of class."

"I'd quit school."

"I'd transfer to another class."

"I'd stay in the class and give you a bad time."

"I'd start bawling."

"I'd want to get even with you."

"But none of you is like that," Miss Alvarez protested.

"We would be if you asked for it," Perry said.

Miss Alvarez laughed. "I hate to say this, but you've made my next point, which is that if I'm hateful you will respond hatefully."

The students looked at her thoughtfully, as if she had said something brand-new.

Miss Alvarez said, "You're thinking that that statement about hatefulness is too simple to be put into words. But it's valid, from the first words the newborn baby hears to the insults nations pass back and forth. Now start listening, because what I'm about to say is probably the most important statement you will ever hear from me: Hurting makes people do things they wouldn't ordinarily do; hurting makes people do things they don't want to do.

"Now back to your assignment. It can be as simple as the way you say something to someone else, or it can be something concrete that you do to improve the world. Let me give you an example. A class of fifth-graders became interested in the problems of the hearing-impaired. They invited a couple of deaf college students to visit their class and to talk in sign language while an interpreter voiced what they were saying.

"There was an immediate kinship between the eager children and the vivacious, enthusiastic deaf visitors. The fifth-graders were especially intrigued when they learned that deaf people can't even order pizza by phone. Imagine a world without pizza delivery! Accordingly, the children wrote a letter to a local pizza establishment explaining the dilemma of deaf pizza lovers. The result was that the phone company provided equipment that enabled the students and the pizza people to exchange typed messages by phone. Also, each of the fifth-graders received a coupon for a large free pizza."

Miss Alvarez cited another illustration, one that has made a major impact on our country's society: "In 1980 thirteen-year-old Cari Lightner was killed by an intoxicated driver. Cari's mother decided to turn her grief and anger into useful channels. With a few friends and her family, Mrs. Lightner organized MADD (Mothers Against Drunk Driving) to reduce alcohol-related deaths and injuries. The movement appealed to thousands of people who were upset by the fact that every twenty-three minutes someone in our country is killed by a drunk driver. During the next few years MADD mushroomed into hundreds of chapters and thousands of volunteers, including SADD (Students Against Driving Drunk). Several of you in this room belong to SADD.

"As a result of one woman's frustration, continuing reforms have been made in legislation, education, and law enforcement. Statistics reveal a significant reduction in alcohol-related motor deaths and injuries."

Miss Alvarez concluded by reminding the students, "This world you live in belongs to you. You have a right to expect a great deal from it, and it has a right to expect much from you. Don't be satisfied with things the way they are. What kind of world do you want for you for your family, and for the children you may someday have?"

The students talked about their expectations: Clean air and water. Food products free of comtaminants. Safety in homes, schools, streets, playgrounds, transportation, the workplace. Freedom of speech, thought, and belief. Respect for individual privacy. Aid from the government when needed, as in the case of disaster, and in matters of poverty, homelessness, and other situations that individuals can't deal with by themselves. In turn, what might society expect from its members? Obedience to law and order. Regard for human rights. Self-care insofar as each person is able. Preservation of human life. Contributions in the way of work and creative efforts. Bringing children into the world in a healthy condition. Participation in community affairs. Loyalty and patriotism. Attempting to make society better by admitting its frailties and working to correct them.

JUST WHAT I NEEDED

Since expectations grow out of needs and desires, we can better understand why others put pressure on us if we give attention to the reasons for their demands.

Perhaps you say something nice to someone: "You look wonderful." "You did a good job on that project." "That was a great meal you cooked." "I'm glad you're here." The response may be, "I needed that." "That's the best thing I've heard all day." "You're just what I need." "You've made my day." The person is saying that you have met one of her or his needs.

You started out with needs the moment you were conceived, and you will continue to have them throughout your life. They fall into two general categories—physical and psychological.

Physical Needs. Your postnatal needs began the moment you were born: oxygen, nourishment, safety, moderate temperature, sleep, and exercise. As infant and child, most of your physical needs were taken care of by others. As you grow older you become more and more responsible for meeting those needs yourself.

Psychological Needs. The needs that affect the way you feel are fully as necessary to health and well-being as are the physical ones. They are part of what makes you human. That is why it is important to know what they are, to be able to talk about them, and to discover ways of dealing with them.

A high school Psychology class was asked to list the five greatest psychological needs. When the lists were combined, the following were ranked highest:

1. Love
2. Security
3. Self-confidence
4. Understanding
5. Trust

Other needs listed were self-esteem, respect, attention, achievement, self-reliance, pride, self-respect. One student mentioned "the need to be noticed." During the course of the discussion, the teacher and students thought of others: the need to learn, to be like other people, to be free from fear, to belong, to be free to express yourself, to feel needed, to be accepted, and to be free from discrimination.

It is difficult to separate some psychological needs. For instance, love and security are closely related. Married people who feel unloved are insecure about their marriage. The infant who has loving, caring parents develops a sense of security and trust. The person who feels needed and has the respect and admiration of others is likely to have self-confidence, self-respect, and self-esteem. A feeling of belonging adds to a sense of security.

Support is another psychological need. Your *support system* is made up of the people in your life to whom you can turn for help. It may include parents and other family members, friends and neighbors, teachers and counselors, and others you feel you can trust and confide in. These are the people who can be relied on from day to day. In addition, everyone sometimes needs help and support from professionals, including doctors and nurses, lawyers, mental health counselors, and social workers.

SPACE NEEDS

We have designated some needs as being physical, others as psychological. One that is both physical and psychological has to do with personal space. Scientists call this need *territoriality*.

People have various ideas about their personal space—how much they need, and when someone intrudes on it. Animals know by instinct the boundaries of their territory and those of others. For example, naturalist Loye Miller studied great horned owls in the San Bernardino Mountains of California. Imitating the owls' calls, he tried to coax them to cross from their homeland into some other owls' hunting territory. The owls refused to trespass. People are not guided by territorial instinct, so must rely on reason and intelligence.

Attitudes about personal space become so much a part of our personalities that feelings and behavior can be affected by trivial incidents. You may become unreasonably annoyed at someone's sitting in your favorite chair or taking your accustomed spot in the school parking lot.

Conflict over space sometimes has to do with trespassing on individual rights. This is expressed in statements such as: "He has no right to put his books in my locker." "My parents don't have the right to listen when I'm on the phone." "My sister leaves her stuff on my side of the room." "The librarian has no right to order me out of the library."

The way we handle space is a way of communicating. The messages our actions convey are often more forceful than words. A student who moves his or her desk against the back wall of the classroom may be expressing a lack of interest in that class. Even if that isn't the message, the teacher may perceive it that way. Every message sent forth means something to the sender. Conflict arises when the receiver of the message "reads" it differently than it was meant.

Perhaps your behavior is affected by space needs that aren't being met. Let's look at some examples of how people and animals are affected by space limitations.

CROWDING

During a fourteen-year study, experimenter John Calhoun allowed a rat colony to become overpopulated. The results were similar to those occurring where overcrowding affects people. The rats developed stress-type illnesses, including heart disease and high blood pressure. The birth rate dropped, and the death rate increased. Mother rats neglected their offspring. Male rats became violent or apathetic.

Because of studies such as Calhoun's, we usually think of crowding as harmful, but in some cases it may be beneficial. Take temperature, for example. Heat worsens the effects of crowding. But what about cold? A group of people plane-wrecked in the Arctic huddle close together for warmth. They are responding to a physical need by crowding together.

When might crowding answer an emotional need? Think of a group of little girls telling ghost stories at a slumber party. As the stories become scarier, the children move closer together.

People attending parades, athletic events, music festivals, games, and circuses tend to cluster close together. In these situations togetherness is part of the fun. Demonstrators, strikers, and other protest groups band together to enhance their effectiveness.

HOW SPACE NEEDS AFFECT BEHAVIOR

The amount of space needed depends on the person, the time, and the situation. Sometimes the need is for absence of space—for body contact with someone or something. A "security blanket" is an object on which a person relies for comfort. Often the object is cuddled or held close to its owner. Close body contact can be a way of expressing love.

No one experiences the same space needs all the time. Just because you want to be by yourself today doesn't mean you always feel that way. For example, Jim comes home from school, goes to his room, and closes the door. His message is, "I need to be by myself." His mother, who has been alone all day, feels shut out and rejected. Her need is for company. Jim's need and his mother's are bumping into each other, and the result is hurtful for both parties. Later, after Jim has had time to himself, he also needs companionship and joins the family.

Some people, however, practically always draw away from companionship or physical contact with others. In extreme cases, avoidance of human contact can result in physical or emotional illness. The ways we relate to people have their roots in infancy and early childhood.

Rita, a high school sophomore, would flinch or cry out when someone touched her. She deliberately kept others at a distance by not bathing, shampooing her hair, brushing her teeth, or wearing clean clothes.

The school counselor learned that the girl's self-damaging behavior was probably the outcome of her earliest childhood. As a baby, Rita had been neglected by her parents and mistreated by foster parents. In fact, she had spent the first two years of her life living in a station wagon with her bitter and frustrated parents. At a time when an infant should have been learning trust and love, Rita was discovering that people can be cold and cruel. As a teenager, Rita lived in a crowded home for unwanted youngsters.

Mrs. Foutz, the school librarian, became interested in Rita after noticing that she spent most of her free time at school reading.

"Rita, how would you like to be a library assistant during your study hall period?" Mrs. Foutz asked one day.

Rita looked suspicious but finally said she would give it a try. Mrs. Foutz gave Rita a considerable amount of work to do, but wisely left her pretty much alone.

One day Rita leaned close to Mrs. Foutz to show her a damaged page in a book.

"Thanks for calling it to my attention," the librarian said. "By the way, you are a great help to me here. How would you like to be stationed at the front desk to check books out to students?"

Rita drew back with a look of panic on her face. "I'd rather just keep on shelving books and doing the bulletin boards."

"Rita, I really need you at the desk this week while Terry's away. All you would have to do is sit behind the desk and stamp the date on the cards."

Reluctantly Rita agreed. Mrs. Foutz noted that Rita did not speak to the students or even look at them as she checked out the books. The third day, however, she did show up in a clean shirt and slacks and with her hair shampooed and neatly brushed.

"You know, you do have pretty hair," Mrs. Foutz mentioned casually. "I never noticed before."

That was the very small beginning of a change in Rita. Gradually she began to visit more with Mrs. Foutz and to answer when the other library assistants spoke to her. By the end of the school year her grooming had noticeably improved. Her grades were better, and her relationships with some teachers were friendly and warm. Sometimes she talked with other students. The lonely space between Rita and the rest of the world was growing smaller.

Many of our problems arise because too much is expected of us. In Rita's case, healthy changes began to take place in her life because someone cared enough about her to expect more of her than she had been willing to give.

THE IMPORTANCE OF NEED FULFILLMENT

Being alive and well does not mean that all of your needs and expectations are fulfilled. You and the people around you are constantly running into frustrations. Frustration occurs when something stands in the way of your needs being met.

For example, Fred's parents are getting a divorce. Fred loves both of them and wants his family to continue as it has been. He feels helpless to do anything about the situation. He is losing a sense of security that has been part of his life.

Mr. Roberts has been a faithful worker on his job for many years. Recently a younger member of the staff was promoted to a position Mr. Roberts felt he deserved. He is experiencing a loss of recognition that he expected from his employer. He feels inadequate as husband and father.

Mrs. Foster has spend her adult life caring for her five children. Now the last of her sons and daughters has left home to go to college. Mrs. Foster no longer feels needed.

Maura failed to make the honor roll for the first time in five and a half years of junior and senior high school. Her pride is hurt, and she is worried about losing the respect and admiration of family, teachers, and classmates who have always expected her to be a top scholar.

We all experience frustration from time to time. It is important to deal with it constructively rather than packing it away inside in the form of anger or a feeling of helplessness. Putting feelings into words is a first step. In addition, we can learn to accept disappointment as a natural part of living and to substitute positive feelings for negative ones by not being too harsh on ourselves.

Spend a few days studying yourself and your family. Try to name one need of each member. Whose need is crashing into someone else's? What are some unpleasant effects on different members of the family? Might some of the needs be met by other members? Note that problems arise when the needs of one person are in conflict with those of another. What kind of compromises might ease some situations within your own family?

Frustration results when needs are not being met. Need fulfillment does not mean always getting what we want.

Dealing with frustration means a willingness to adjust to those roadblocks that we can't overcome. Human conflict results when our needs are not the same as the other person's. Getting along means taking other people's desires into consideration along with our own.

CHAPTER 4

So Who Are
You, Really?

The question, "Who are you?" was posed to a class of fourth-graders. They were told to answer it by completing the statement, "I am..." with the first three things that came to mind. All but a few answers were definite and uncomplicated. Among the most common responses were the child's name, sex, and status in society: "I am a girl in Mr. Allen's fourth grade." "I am a Boy Scout." Several pupils mentioned nationality or race: "I am an American." "I am Chicano." Some reflected a sense of selfness: "I am me." Almost without exception, the statments answered the question "Who?"

A group of adults, given the same assignment, also told who they considered themselves to be: "I am Marty's parent," "...an accountant," "...a student at the university."

When instructed to say who they were, teenagers didn't answer the question in the same way. Instead, they often responded with "how-I-am" answers. Out of three hundred responses from students in one high school, fewer than half were "who" answers. The majority were reflections of feelings. They included: stupid, crazy, worthless, happy, honest, bored, depressed, self-conscious, lonely, easygoing, mixed-up.

What might we conclude from the way teenagers see themselves compared to the way children and adults do? Perhaps the teens' identifications reflect feelings of confusion. Adolescents may not be sure *who* they are at this period in their lives. The uncertainty is caused partly by the many chemical alterations taking place in the adolescent body, which can result in up-and-down mood swings.

The teen years are a time of seesawing between the desire to remain a protected child and a longing to be an adult in charge of one's own life. According to psychologist Erik Erikson, the most important task of adolescence is to find a satisfying answer to the question, "Who am I?"

YOU: HOW DID YOU GET THIS WAY?

Teenager Bart tells his parents jokingly, "Whatever's wrong with me has to be your fault because I'm the sum of my heredity and my environment."

Although Bart's parents aren't about to accept the blame for all of his shortcomings, he is right that who you are depends on a combination of factors—your heredity (including some temperamental tendencies), your physical and emotional state during your mother's pregnancy, the events that occurred at the time of your birth, and all that has happened to you since.

You may feel that you are "stuck" with your heredity. Consider, however, the power that environment has to shape that inheritance. Take height, for instance. Although heredity may have the power to make you six feet tall, you could wind up shorter through injury, illness, malnutrition, glandular malfunction, or even emotional causes. You might be born with musical aptitude, yet never become a musician because of lack of interest, encouragement, money, training, or self-confidence.

You are made up of thousands of ingredients—physical, mental, and emotional. Some you can mold; others are beyond your control. However, so many combinations are possible that you can create someone wonderful. A human being is too complicated to be simply a blob, a zero, a nobody, or a loser. Any day is an ideal time to start rearranging all those pieces of you into a satisfying whole.

WHO OWNS YOU?

Do you ever wonder, "How can I be me and at the same time the person others want me to be?"

A great deal of the who-am-I? confusion is the result of the many expectations of the people in your life. Then there's the problem of being an individual while conforming to society's expectations. Students in a Human Behavior class talked about the expectations placed on them: "My dad thinks I'm smarter than I am." "My girlfriend expects me to spend all my spare time with her." "Every teacher piles a ton of homework on us every day."

It is no wonder if you sometimes feel like a marionette being manipulated by others. Who does all this expecting?

Society. Besides being governed by so many laws that you can't be familiar with all of them, you are subject to the mores—that is, customs—of a given segment of society. For instance, it is law that citizens must pay taxes. Although it is not law, it is an expectation that adults be self-supporting.

Parents. Parental goals began during your infancy with expecting you to sleep through the night without having to be fed. Family expectations have been going on ever since.

Teachers and Other Youth Leaders. Think back on all those volumes of knowledge packed into your brain—the academics, those knots you learned to tie in Scout troop, the piano lessons, the athletic skills, the social graces. You keep learning and performing because of the expectations of various people in your life.

Peers. Often those expecting people are members of your own age group. They urge, "Let's throw a party." "Join the chess club." "Let's go steady." "Shape up." "Don't listen to your parents."

Self. Sometimes that someone is you. You want to make your parents proud of you. You decide to go to college. You'd like to be the fastest runner in the school. You want to improve your grades. You will look better after you lose that extra weight.

In the long run, it is the expectations of family—especially parents—that impose the most constant pressure. Somehow you must learn to handle those gracefully while fitting the expectations of others into your total life pattern. For expectations to be reasonable, they must be within the reach of the person's abilities. At each age a person is able to do some things and not others. For instance, a child won't speak in sentences before having a sizable vocabulary of single words. You won't play in the school band until you have learned to read music.

YOUR VALUES

Value system is one of the most important shapers of personality. Values are the standards we live by. They, in turn, grow out of our philosophies—what we believe.

A family's value system has much to do with the way its members cope with problems. Vince, the son of an alcoholic father and a submissive mother, is more likely to learn a pattern of avoidance than if his parents dealt with crises in a mature fashion. In general, families tend to adopt the customs and beliefs of their society, and individuals tend to grow up with the beliefs of their parents.

But wait! While you were a child, what your parents and teachers said made pretty good sense. Then gradually you began to experience a preteen restlessness. You found yourself questioning some of the wisdom of those adults. Who were you, anyway? As an adolescent you had reached a scary time in your life, afraid of being merely a shadow of those grown-ups and also afraid of being turned loose without their protection.

What you may not have realized was that those parents were also experiencing fear—fear of losing control of you, their most remarkable creation.

When values and philosophies among people clash, the result can be panic, or at least unrest. Individual philosophies often differ from those of society. Your state may believe in capital punishment but you do not. You may not go along with all the tenets of your religion; for instance, you may accept the concept of divorce although your church does not. Your beliefs probably won't always be the same as those of your parents. They may feel that everyone should have a college education, but you want to join the military or become a chef.

Values vary greatly from family to family. Most families

stress honesty as a desirable characteristic, but interpretations of honesty differ. Dorene's parents, for instance, have taught her from early childhood that it is wrong to lie. However, when Dorene missed school to go on a camping trip, her mother "covered" for her by saying she was ill. Sylvia's parents, on the other hand, would not make an excuse for their daughter who was on the same trip. Their philosophy is that Sylvia should pay the penalty for her unexcused absence from school.

PARENTS AND KIDS—DIFFERENT WAVELENGTHS

Adolescent behavior that comes across as rebellion may actually be the young person's reaction to pressure. According to studies by psychologists and psychiatrists, adolescents are subject to considerable stress, no matter what their circumstances.

It is normal for the teenager's feelings of happiness and optimism to alternate with periods of depression and hopelessness. The body is undergoing drastic physical and emotional changes at the same time that the world is moving ahead at an alarming rate. Adolescence is "in-betweenhood." No wonder the high-schooler keeps wondering, "Who am I?"

Perry Grayling says of himself, "The more I learn about myself, the more I think my parents always expected me to act like a child, so I did. When I got to junior high school, I still acted childish, so my teachers expected me to. The kids did, too. I figured I had to show off for them."

That little-boy image followed Perry to high school. Fortunately, teachers and classmates there expected more grown-up behavior from him. Now Perry is working toward meeting that expectation.

Perry's "self-fulfilling-prophecy" attitude has been demonstrated among animals as well as people. In one study, psychologist Robert Rosenthal divided college students into two groups. Both groups were given ordinary laboratory rats for an experiment. One group was told that they were dealing with "especially intelligent" rats; the other, with rats that were "dull." Both groups were instructed to "teach the rats what you can." Guess which rats learned the tricks. The so-called bright ones, of course.

Similar experiments have been done with students, who are selected at random rather than according to actual ability. The children who are labeled "gifted" or "above-average" learn more than students labeled "average or below."

One educator defined self-fulfilling prophecy as "not what *I* think I am, and not what *you* think I am, but what *I* think *you* think I am." In other words, it is not self-image that is the influential factor, but your perception of how others judge you.

WHERE ARE YOU GOING, AND WHY?

Motivation and goals are a major cause of conflict between parents and teenagers. Why? Behavior is largely the result of what we have planned for ourselves. Youngsters are inclined to think in terms of the present and immediate future. The younger and more immature the person, the more instant the demand. The baby's main concern may be how fast the parent can transfer a spoonful of food from dish to baby's mouth. The preschooler looks forward to being read to at bedtime. The school-age child anticipates the end of the school day, a coming birthday party, Christmas. The adolescent is preoccupied with now, and also with the goal of graduating from high school. Some think of future

Loretta's compulsiveness may have its roots in her early upbringing. Her parents were killed in an auto accident when she was two years old. She was raised by a spinster aunt who was conscientious and kind but not accustomed to being around children. Aunt Betsy knew how to discipline but not how to let a child be a child. She constantly corrected Loretta for behavior that was normal for her age. "Let's be a little lady," was a familiar reminder. If Loretta's bed wasn't made faultlessly, she had to make it over. Mistakes in homework had to be corrected immediately. Loretta grew up with the idea that "normal" means "perfect."

Loretta is highly intelligent and willing to make sacrifices to reach lofty goals. However, she has difficulty adjusting to the mistakes of others and to her own imperfections. She suffers from migraine headaches when things don't go as planned, and she can't forgive herself for errors that she considers "foolish" or "stupid."

It is possible that Loretta is so dedicated to becoming a physician that she loses touch with the steps involved in fulfilling her dream. Certainly she is pursuing her short-term and intermediate objectives by being a dedicated student. She may be overlooking the truth that constant perfection is unnatural. Short-term and intermediate steps are a training ground, complete with mistakes, failures, and disappointments. Mistakes are part of the learning process.

What will happen to Loretta's self-concept if she is not accepted into medical school? If she becomes a doctor and has trouble getting into a practice that suits her to perfection? If she becomes a doctor and her patients find her not as human and sympathetic as they might wish? If she is overwhelmed by risks such as making a mistake where a patient's health or life is at stake, or possible malpractice suits?

No matter what a person's ambition, it is healthy to be able to settle for second-best when dreams don't become reality.

Many teenagers are not as certain as Loretta about long-range goals. In fact, most college students change their major at least once. Between now and the time you are ready for a career, the world will have changed greatly, opening up opportunities you may never have dreamed of. So how can you decide on short-term and intermediate goals?

Don't be one of those adults who look back with laments such as, "I wish I had gotten better grades in school." "I wish someone had made me take more math." "I wish I had gone to college or trade school." "I wish I had given more thought to the future."

Be on the safe side by taking useful subjects, by learning salable skills either in school or on the job, and by deciding on education and training beyond high school. Good grades in high school may help to open exciting doors later on. In the meantime, your best preparation for the future is to do a good job of living each day, and that, of course, includes successful human relationships.

WHO IS THAT WEIRD PERSON IN THE MIRROR?

The self you want the world to see is your *surface image*, sometimes called "public image." One teenager described it as "that part of you who dresses up for company." *Self-image* is the way you see yourself. If self-image is considerably different from surface image, you are likely to come across as "phony." That occurs when people don't like their real self, so pretend to be someone they are not.

Self-image is a combination of emotional and physical features. Some people say looks don't count; it's who you are that matters. When reminded by her mother that "beauty is only skin deep," teenage Susie replied, "But it's my skin people are looking at, not my soul."

The way you look is indeed part of your personality. But how you *think* you look is even more significant than how you do look. The way you think of yourself as looking affects the way you feel about yourself. It works the other way around, too. The way you feel about yourself affects the way you think you look. Looks plus feelings about self equal self-image.

Dr. Maxwell Maltz, a plastic surgeon, sees self-image as a key to success or failure. According to him, that doesn't mean physical appearance only; there is need to heal inner scars as well as external ones. Patients with a low opinion of themselves sometimes do not see improvement in their looks following successful plastic surgery because they don't *feel* better than they did before. How does one go about healing emotional wounds? Dr. Maltz's recommendation is to forgive others and to forgive yourself. Stop imitating others and be yourself.

For now, your task is to get acquainted with that perplexing person who is you.

CHAPTER ◇ 5

Parents and Those Other People in Your Life

For his term project in Adolescent Psychology, Clayton Porter decided to write about the major relationships in his life. As a beginning, he listed some of the roles he plays: son, stepson, brother, student, classmate, friend, neighbor, Key Club president, guitarist, Mindy's boyfriend, employee, member of the swimming team, student council member.

"It's hard playing all those different roles," Clay wrote. "Makes me feel sort of like an actor. We teenagers want to be ourselves, but sometimes when we are, we land in trouble. For instance, this morning Dad yelled at me for chewing gum and having my cap on in front of company last night. I explained that's

just being me, and he said, 'Well, start being some-
body else when company's here!'"

Clay's teacher Mr. Gorski explained that changing roles
does not mean being artificial; it simply means adjusting
our personality to what's going on at a given time. The
adults in your life tend to judge behavior as right or wrong,
good or bad. Your ideas of right and wrong aren't always
the same as someone else's. A more practical word to
use might be "appropriate." Appropriate appearance,
language, or behavior is that which fits in comfortably. You
can tailor your role to what is acceptable for the situation.
For instance, you wouldn't show up for a job interview in a
sweat suit. You don't talk in the classroom the way you do
with friends. You treat your sister or brother differently
than you do your girlfriend or boyfriend.

"I know this paper is supposed to be about *human*
relations," Clay wrote, "but I have to mention my
dog, Sambo, as someone really important in my life.
What's great about Sambo is that he's always around. I
can count on him. He never bawls me out. He's glad
to see me even when I'm in a rotten mood. He doesn't
boss me, and he doesn't care whether my room's clean
or not. Also, he doesn't rat on me or give away my
secrets. I guess you could say we love each other.

"But about the people in my life—I love some of
them, too. As Mr. Gorski says, though, love gets
tangled up with a lot of other feelings. Emotions
travel in bunches, he says.

"My dad—Naturally I love him and respect him a
lot. The problem is he has always come down on me
really hard. Because he's a colonel in the military, he's
used to giving orders and being obeyed. This class has

helped me realize that that's why I have some bad feelings about authority figures such as teachers, parents, and cops. One day Mr. Gorski said something that made me realize that the way I treat teachers—especially men—is a reflection of the way I feel about Dad. I came into class and slouched down in my seat as usual and started looking bored. Mr. Gorski said, 'Clayton, I don't know what you're hacked off about, but I haven't done anything to deserve your insolence, so save your bad manners for the person you're upset with.'

"That embarrassed me and made me mad, but it also made me see myself more clearly. I thought a lot about Dad, too. He was raised by a super strict father who punished him often. Maybe that's why Dad joined the military, so he could boss other people around. Miss Alvarez, our Family Living teacher, says parents tend to be like their own parents unless they learn better ways."

Clay's teacher is right about parenting patterns passing from generation to generation. Studies of rhesus monkeys at the primate laboratory of the University of Wisconsin indicate that monkeys who did not have normal mothering in infancy grow up to be neglectful and abusive of their own babies. People, as well as monkeys, learn behavior patterns from their parents. During the 1960s a systematic study was made of characteristics of abusive mothers. Three of those traits were outstanding:

1. The abusive parents considered brutal punishment an acceptable method of discipline.
2. They expected too much of their children and viewed them as bad.

3. They had a background of abuse in their own
   childhood.

In another study of sixty families, psychiatrists Steele and Pollock of the University of Colorado discovered that a characteristic of battering parents was that as children they had been abused or emotionally mistreated. All had been subjected to continuous demands and criticisms from their parents.

Family-life experts are in firm agreement that people who are successful parents usually had tender, loving parents. Furthermore, research indicates that babies who are given an abundance of parental love and attention during infancy become self-assured and independent earlier than babies who are ignored.

Clay described his relationship with his stepmother in these words:

> "I think if I look at my stepmother fairly I would have
> to say she is an okay person. But instead of accepting
> her for who she is, my feelings keep getting in the
> way. You see, Mom has been dead less than a year. I
> realize that Dad needs someone to keep house and be
> a wife to him and a mother to Kenny and me, but I
> resent Grace for being where my mother ought to be.
> I'm angry at Dad for marrying so soon. Well, anyway,
> I keep telling myself that I don't hate Grace. She's
> good to me and tries to act like a mother, but she's
> never had kids of her own, so she thinks she's sup-
> posed to treat me like a ten-year-old. Really bugs me!"

Clay probably doesn't realize that he is still going through the grief process over the loss of his mother, and that one aspect of grief is anger. It is normal to feel angry, even at the person who has died. If Clay were to admit this anger to himself, he would feel guilty. It is easier to visit his frustration on the people in his life who are still alive.

> "I honestly wouldn't want to be an only child, but lately Kenny, my eleven-year-old brother, has been getting on my nerves. I can't blame Dad and Grace for playing favorites, I guess. After all, Ken does everything he's told to do and is so agreeable it makes me want to throw up. Somehow I get this feeling it's all put on, though. He just can't be that satisfied with always being bossed around, and by a stepmother at that. Why can't Kenny just act normal and cry or yell or have a tantrum once in a while so I could really light in on him? As it is, I'm expected to treat him like he's something special, and my parents think he is."

Clay's jealousy is showing in that passage, but he may have good reason for concern. He sees his brother as too good to be true. Kenny's exaggerated obedience and cooperation may hide some unpleasant feelings that he thinks he shouldn't express. His efforts to please his parents may also be a way of trying to replace the mother he has lost. Family members have different ways of handling crises. Clayton's being able to admit his negative feelings may be healthier than Kenny's "everything's-all-right" attitude.

Clay's feelings toward teachers were expressed as follows:

> "I never really thought of teachers as people. They were just someone to boss me around and try to make me learn. My grade-school teachers were mostly women who fussed over the kids like mothers. It wasn't until junior high that I started getting men

teachers. I developed a big fat dislike for my wood-shop teacher, who was strict like my father. I realize now he had to put the screws on us so we wouldn't goof around and get hurt on the equipment. At the time, though, he was just one more boss in my life—one more father. At first in high school I refused to work in a class if I didn't like the teacher. After I flunked a few courses, I got some smarts and realized I was hurting myself instead of getting even with the teacher. I've finally learned to separate the subject matter from my feelings about teachers. Now I do most of the assignments."

It is perceptive of Clayton to recognize that his negative attitude toward some teachers began with unhappy relationships he experienced during his growing-up years. Knowing this can help him think of educators as individuals to be liked or appreciated as ordinary people.

Clay wrote about other authority figures:

"When I was a little kid, I thought Dad was an ogre because he was so strict. He wasn't a child beater, but he did spank me pretty often. My mother interfered and said something like, 'He's only a little boy, Malcolm.' Maybe that's why I miss her so much. She was a cushion between me and Dad. Maybe one reason Kenny tries so hard to be good is that he's afraid Dad will come down on him the way he does on me. Perhaps he's playing it smart. Maybe I wish Dad would hit him once in a while so I'd be sure he doesn't like Ken better than he does me. Anyhow, I get nervous when I'm around the principal or vice principal at school. That's really dumb because they're pleasant and friendly enough. They even treat me fairly when I'm sent to the office for doing something I shouldn't. As for cops, I used to get paranoid just thinking about them. Then my motorcycle was stolen and I had to report it to the police. They were helpful and didn't give up until they located the cycle. That made me see them as just people with a job to do. I even thought of them as the police instead of the 'pigs'."

A certain resistance to authority is normal. A basic human need is to exercise control. Thus, the person in authority is fulfilling a need by controlling others. The one being controlled, on the other hand, may develop resentment at the loss of his or her own mastery over a situation. Clayton said of his peers:

"I get along okay with kids my own age. My parents don't approve of some of my friends, but as long as I stay out of trouble they don't order me to keep away from anyone in particular. I know Dad would like to lay down the law about that, but I think he's a little afraid of losing control over me if he gets too harsh.

"I'm having problems with my girlfriend lately. She gets pretty hacked off when I go out of town to a ball game or spend an evening with the guys. When I tell her she doesn't own me, she sulks or cries to make me feel guilty. The trouble is, she's really something and I don't want to lose her, but I don't want her deciding what I ought to do, either. One stepmother is enough."

Although love relationships begin with our parents, human development is not complete until we can gain satisfaction from our peers. Even though some of Clay's negative feelings from past experiences spill over onto his present relationships, he expresses a need for friendships in his own age group.

Researchers at the University of Wisconsin studied this need in a group of monkeys. The baby animals spent their early weeks largely in contact with their mother. By one month of age the babies were leaving their mother for brief periods to explore their surroundings. During the second month the infants spent increasing amounts of time away from their mothers and were exposed to other monkeys of their age. By three months they were seeking out age-mates to play with, and at four months they were engaging in regular social activity among their peers. Human children don't mature as fast as monkeys, but they, too, reach a stage of social development when they need interaction with peers.

Clayton described some of his on-the-job conflicts.

"Teenagers always need money for things like dates, cars, class rings, proms, ski trips. Most of us don't have parents who can afford to dish out all that cash. Chances are, they wouldn't anyway. 'We had to work for everything we got,' my parents are always saying. Anyway, I don't want them to give me all the money I need for extras. That wouldn't be fair, and besides, they really would own me then. The answer to the problem is to land a job, which sounds pretty simple until you get turned down a few times.

"The jobs we finally get aren't all that inspiring. Our Distributive Education teacher calls them 'entry' jobs—jobs we work at until we get the education and training we need for a career. My entry job is turning out pizzas by the hundreds to a complaining public. It's not exactly like those scenes on TV commercials where the workers line up and sing joyful songs to the smiling customers. I tried three jobs before I realized that working for someone else is serious business. I found out the meaning of the old saying, 'The customer is always right.' So is the boss, it turns out. I had a habit of dropping classes at school when they didn't suit me, but that doesn't work so well with a job. I gave up clerking at a drugstore because the boss wouldn't give me time off to go on a club trip. I soon found out it wasn't too easy to get another job. Employers aren't dying to take on a kid who quit somewhere else a few weeks after being hired. Then I got fired from a filling-station job for not calling in when I was sick. I finally learned that there are times when I have to take orders from other people. There's one big startling difference between a boss and the other authority figures in your life. Parents, teachers, camp directors, Scout leaders, probation officers, and other people like that are trying to do something to benefit the child or young person. Employers, on the other hand, have their own interests at heart. Not that most bosses don't take an interest in their employees, but in the long run they are out to make a living, so the employees serve *them* instead of the other way around."

SO WHAT TO DO ABOUT IT ?

Clayton concluded his paper as follows:

"I know Mr. Gorski won't consider this project completed until I apply what I've written to my own life. He says we students are forever complaining about our classes not being relevant. He says it's up to us to make them relevant. The purpose of knowedge, he insists, is to help us do a better job of living.

"So here's my summary: Writing about yourself and the people in your life helps you to know yourself better as well as those others. One of the things this paper helped me realize is that the relationship you have with someone can affect how you get along with others. I think the lesson from that is that you have to accept everyone for himself or herself and not get the person mixed up with someone else you've known. I also got a better understanding of how other people feel. Consider my stepmother, for instance. She's probably having a hard time accepting me and Ken, especially me. I began to see things from the boss's viewpoint, too. He's not there to try to understand me or to worry about my warped feelings. He hired me to serve his needs. Writing the paper gave me a new look at Mindy, my girl. She tends to be possessive, and that's not good for a relationship. Somehow I need to be assertive and stand up for my rights without driving her away.

"I think from now on I will pay more attention to how I get along with people and try to see things from their point of view. Sometimes my stepmother talks about 'mending fences.' I think she means straightening out differences and getting back on peaceful terms with someone. Maybe she and I have some fences to mend."

Of course, not everyone has the same people problems as Clayton, but all of us experience some uncomfortable human relationships at times because of the differences among people. Therapists and counselors are aware that helping to solve problems depends on their clients' understanding of other people's needs, as well as learning to communicate their own.

BEING VALUABLE

A valuable person is one who is appreciated by others. If we appreciate someone, we usually also like that person. What are the qualities that make us liked by others?

Let's go back to Clayton's remarks about his dog. Why did he choose to describe his relationship with Sambo? Probably because his pet possesses qualities that Clay would like for people to have. Which ones did Clay mention?

Being Available. Sambo is always around. In other words, Clay can count on him. We need people in our lives to whom we can turn—someone standing by, a support system of people who are there when we need them. When asked what he wanted of his parents, one teenager answered, "I just want them to be there—not hovering over me, but handy when I need them."

Being Appreciated. Clay said that Sambo never bawls him out. Probably none of us gets through a week without being chastised or criticized. But if we get more negative than positive feedback from others, we begin to doubt our own worth. One way you can be valuable to your family and others is to remember to comment on favorable things about them.

You Love Me Anyway. Clay says Sambo is glad to see him even when he's in a rotten mood. People tend to reject us when we are being our old ugly selves. You will be a precious person if you can like people when they are at their worst. The more unlovable a person is, the more love she or he needs.

Letting People Be Who They Are.   Clay's dog doesn't boss him around. He doesn't try to change him. Sambo accepts Clay as he is. A major conflict between people arises because each of us knows how others ought to be. If people would only follow our advice and do things our way, we think, the world would be practically perfect. Sambo will settle for Clayton exactly the way he is

I Can Trust You.   One of Sambo's great qualities is that he can keep a secret. How often we wish we could share a confidence with someone but don't dare because we can't think of anyone who can resist telling just one more person. Your list of friends will grow if people discover that you are one of the few who can guard a secret.

WHAT TEENAGERS LIKE IN OTHERS

Students in Home Economics classes were asked to mention someone they especially liked, not by name, but by relationship, and give the most outstanding reason for liking the person. Among the responses were the following:

Stepmother. Shows she cares about me.
Brother. Makes me feel important.
Friend. I can tell him everything.
Best friend. Lets me be me.
Teacher. Always willing to help me.
Cousin. Has a sense of humor. Lets me act the way I want.
Boyfriend. Respects me. Is careful of my feelings.
Father. When things go bad, he's always there.

Older brother. Cares what I do with my life.

Friend. Never makes fun of people.

Foster mother. Seems glad to have me. Listens to me.

Priest. Good sense of humor. Understands young people.

Uncle. Warm and caring.

Mother. Easy to talk to.

Parents. Make me grow up and do things on my own.

School principal. Firm, but kind and understanding.

School counselor. Makes me feel like someone.

Those are only a sampling of the responses, but certain qualities were mentioned again and again: Is caring. Is understanding. Listens. Is helpful. Lets me be myself. Can be counted on. Makes me feel all right about myself. Only one student mentioned physical appearance; she said she likes her boyfriend because he is "handsome and considerate."

The marvelous feature about the characteristics mentioned is that they are available to all of us. Some assets, such as intelligence, talent, and physical attributes, depend largely on heredity. But the ways in which we relate to people are acquired traits, not inborn. They can be developed, beginning at any time.

CHAPTER 6

What's Your

Message?

During a discussion in Psychology class, Perry Grayling remarked, "If it weren't for other people, I'd get along just fine."

Mr. Gorski said, "Your remark reflects two key reasons for our difficulties in working out human relationships. We think we are right, which makes it difficult to appreciate the other person's viewpoint. Second, we are so preoccupied with our own side of the issue that we have trouble listening to anyone who disagrees."

Class members had much to say on the subject of being listened to.

Duane commented, "When Dad and I have an argument, I can tell he isn't listening. He's figuring out what he's going to say as soon as I stop talking."

After several minutes of discussion, Mr. Gorski summed up the students' comments. "What you are saying is that people don't listen to you. Will you admit that others could say the same thing about you?"

Some students admitted being poor listeners at times.

Mr. Gorski said, "Besides the problem of listening and being listened to, let's think about other factors that interfere with smooth human relationships. On a piece of paper jot down things that come to mind that describe why people have trouble getting along. Don't bother with complete sentences."

Student comments included the following:

People disliking each other.
Not being able to trust someone, or someone not trusting you.
Getting cut down.
Getting your feelings hurt.
People trying to own me, trying to run my life.
Not being able to accept differences among people.
"Using" other people for your own gain.
Not letting me be myself. Trying to make me over.
Being jealous.
Being critical.
Lack of communication.
Saying one thing *to* me and something else *about* me.

Notice that the obstacles the students saw involve emotions: anger, resentment, jealousy, hurt, mistrust, suspicion. Furthermore, the persons in a relationship experience different feelings. Suppose, for example, Melanie feels angry and jealous because her boyfriend, Reese, shows an interest in her girlfriend, Ginny. Although Reese is in love with Melanie, he resents her possessiveness. Also, he feels a growing interest in Ginny. Ginny is attracted to Reese but at the same time is upset over Melanie's coldness toward her.

Human relations are not handled simply through our

being reasonable and rational. Those bothersome feelings keep getting in the way.

HOW DO *YOU* COMMUNICATE?

A common complaint people have of one another is "lack of communication." Actually there is seldom an absence of communication, but although it exists, it may not be of a satisfying quality.

Communication means an exchange of messages. A message must not only be sent, but received. We ordinarily think of communication as involving language. However, the sending and receiving of messages does not have to be with words. We communicate through actions, gestures, facial expressions, clothing, posture, and silence.

Spend a few days observing people. Notice what they are "saying" without words. It is said that "actions speak louder than words." When what a person says does not agree with what he or she does, we are likely to believe the behavior rather than the words. A third-grader told his parents, "That baby-sitter tells us that she likes us, but she doesn't act like it."

Movies, articles, stories, and books often deal with human relationships that have become twisted or broken. In many cases, the tragedy could have been avoided through clear and honest communication. A television talk show was devoted to unfulfilled expectations of adult sons and daughters and their mothers. "We communicate all right," a divorced woman said of her relationship with her thirty-four-old son, "but we fight all the time."

Another mother said, "At least you talk to each other. My daughter and I don't even speak."

"When you do speak, it's to criticize me," the daughter accused.

Another daughter complained that her mother had never been around to listen to her when she, the daughter, was a child. "I never dreamed you felt neglected," her mother said.

In short, during the hour-long program these people and others put into words hurts that had been festering inside of them for years.

WHY WON'T THE WORDS COME OUT?

Asked why they find it difficult to discuss problems with their families, Miss Alvarez's Family Living class members wrote the following comments:

I'm scared of my folks. I plan what I'll say, but when the chance comes, the words just won't come out.

My parents keep talking about divorce, and I'm afraid of pushing things over the brink.

My family doesn't believe in talking about our problems.

I can't get anyone to pay attention to what I say. People don't take me seriously.

When I bring up anything unpleasant, my parents get the wrong idea. It's like we're on different wavelengths.

Miss Alvarez said, "I think it's time for us to learn to do some thinking around corners. When we think about the future, we tend to look straight ahead as if we are in a tunnel and no other direction is available. Often the scene at the end of the tunnel is bleak, but we figure there's nothing we can do about it. This is especially true in the matter of communication. Because we have had a bad experience in trying to get through to someone, we assume there's no point in trying.

"Suppose we play a game of 'What if—.' What if I say whatever I feel like saying to my parents even if I'm afraid they'll get mad? What if I say something in a startling way to get the listener's attention? What if I say something in a different way than usual—a way that isn't so likely to upset people? Why don't I insist on talking about a problem even if my family doesn't think I should? Why don't I tell my parents I'm worried about their getting a divorce?"

The class members looked skeptical.

Miss Alvarez said, "See what I mean? You hesitate to try something new. It would be taking a risk, wouldn't it?"

"It might work, though," Jessica said. "Since I got assertive about keeping in contact with my father, Mom and I can at least talk about it, and she does let Dad and me keep in touch, although she still doesn't think it's a good idea."

"I believe I'll turn this into an assignment," Miss Alvarez decided.

The class laughed good-naturedly. "We thought you might," Roy said.

"Since you're all so agreeable, try this. Think of something concerning a family matter that you would like to talk about but haven't had the courage to bring up. Then force yourself to state your comment to a member or members of the family. Write a summary of the family's reactions and the results of your attempt."

Perry sighed. "In case I'm not in class tomorrow, you'll know I carried out the assignment and got killed."

"Poor kid," Miss Alvarez said. "Now, if we're going to be brave enough to actually talk to our families, perhaps we should adopt some rules to make the task more likely to be successful."

The class finally came up with the following list:

1. Don't accuse or blame the people in your family.
2. Assume part of the blame yourself, even if you don't think you are at fault.
3. Talk about your feelings rather than about what people are doing to you.
4. Be in charge of your emotions.
5. Keep your voice down.
6. Build up people's feelings about themselves.
7. Be prepared to make some compromises.

Miss Alvarez was pleased with the suggestions. She said, "I'll add one you might want to try: Plant seeds in people's minds." In answer to the puzzled expressions on the students' faces, she added, "When people are in a state of turmoil, they don't listen very well. They certainly don't follow advice all of a sudden. Remember that if your family is troubled and if what you say to them has an upsetting effect, their reactions may be unreasonable, defensive, or quarrelsome. They may get angry or deny what you're saying. However, what you say may take root. Someday, later on, it may sprout and be accepted.

"For instance, suppose you say, 'Please don't treat me like a child. I need some room to grow.' Your parents probably aren't going to say, 'Of course you're not a child. We'll start increasing your privileges tomorrow.'"

The class laughed at the absurdity of that possibility.

"However," Miss Alvarez went on, "if you continue to act responsibly over time, your thought may take shape in your parents' minds and they may accept it. They may even think it was their idea."

HOW CAN I TELL YOU WHAT I MEAN?

Human behaviorists agree that communication is the number one key in human relationships. We often say to one another, "Come on, level with me." What we mean is, don't lie to me, or don't shut me off. Why is it so difficult to do that, to come right out and say what we mean? We simply haven't learned how. Counselors deal with numerous problems involving people who don't know how to level with others.

In discussing his problems with the school counselor, Vince described his family life as "a disaster" because of his father's alcoholism.

"What does that have to do with your being in trouble with the law?" Mr. Rudolph asked.

Vince said, "I get so frustrated I just wind up doing all kinds of things I shouldn't."

"For instance?" the counselor prompted.

"Like skipping school and getting hung up on drugs. Wrecking Dad's pickup."

"Did you ever tell your father how you feel about his drinking?" Mr. Rudolph asked.

"He knows. I've tried everything."

"What does 'everything' include, Vince?"

Vince frowned and fidgeted in his chair before answering. "Well, I used to go along with everything he said, even when it was unreasonable."

"Why did you do that?" Mr. Rudolph asked.

"I was scared not to. It didn't work, though. Dad still yelled at me for everything. He's pretty ugly when he's drunk."

"Did you feel better while you were trying to be agreeable?"

"No. I was steaming inside."

"So what did you try next?"

"I completely ignored Dad. Just walked out on him whenever he started yelling at Mom and me."

"That didn't work, either, did it?"

Vince looked surprised. "No. How did you know?"

Mr. Rudolph said, "You can't solve a problem by pretending it doesn't exist. I imagine your father's behavior got worse when you ignored him, didn't it?"

Vince nodded vigorously. "That's for sure! So then I started yelling back and refusing to do what he said. Dad got so mad he hit me. That's when I left home and wound up at the Youth Crisis Center. That really brought the roof down. Dad and Mom sent the police after me."

"And you've been in and out of trouble ever since," the counselor summed up.

"*In*, anyway," Vince agreed.

Mr. Rudolph said, "Behavior is a form of communication, a reflection of how we feel. What message were you trying to get across to your parents?"

"That I can't stand living in a house with a drunken father and a mother who takes any abuse he dishes out."

"Did you tell your parents that?"

"Not in so many words," Vince admitted.

"Why not?"

Vince looked surprised at the question. "I was afraid to. You can't just come out and say something like, 'Dad, I'm fed up with your boozing. Mom, I'm sick of your being a doormat.'"

"Why couldn't you say that, Vince?"

"Well look, Mr. Rudolph, what do you think would happen if I said something like that?"

"Nothing pleasant," the counselor admitted.

Vince looked thoughtful for a few minutes before speaking again. "But you still think I should tell them that?"

Mr. Rudolph leaned forward and put his hand on Vince's arm. "You've been telling them that all along through your misbehavior, the anger in your voice and expression, your leaving home. The results were painful, so you would have no more to be afraid of by putting your feelings into honest, straightforward language."

"Nothing would change," Vince countered.

"Perhaps not. However, expressing feelings verbally drains off some of the steam. If you had spoken up, you might not have had to express your rage in actions. You might have saved yourself some punishment. That's what leveling with your folks might do for you. It might also do something for them."

"Like what?" Vince wanted to know.

"Like telling them plainly exactly where you stand. For example, 'Dad, I know I can't do anything about your drinking, and Mom, I can't tell you how to handle your problems, but I've got to get out of this kind of life.'"

"What would that accomplish?"

"It would explain why you have been acting badly. It would tell them you are concerned about what they are doing to you and to themselves. It would give them something new to think about, a new way of looking at the family."

"And if they didn't change?"

"That would be their problem, Vince, but at least they would understand your reason for leaving home if, and when, you do."

After several visits with the counselor, Vince decided that talking with his parents would be no worse than what was going on already.

As expected, the talk wasn't pleasant. Vince's father flew into a rage and "yelled his way around the house," as Vince expressed it. However, Vince's father did blurt out his own frustrations and complaints against his wife and son. He talked about a lifetime of "bum deals" that had contributed to his drinking. Vince's mother for the first time did a little yelling of her own. She expressed how it felt to be married to a constant drinker and to be the mother of a sullen boy usually in trouble.

"At least we know each other better now," Vince confided when describing the scene to Mr. Rudolph. "I see myself as a pretty hateful character, too. Maybe we can change; who knows? At least maybe *I* can change."

Once Vince had decided to practice leveling with his parents, he and Mr. Rudolph talked about finding better ways to put his feelings into words: "Dad, I worry about your drinking. We learned at school that heavy drinking is a health problem. I am upset about what is happening to our family. We don't show that we care about each other. We don't act like a family. Mom, I wish you'd get out of the house more and do things with your friends. You should make a life of your own instead of fretting about Dad and me all the time."

At Mr. Rudolph's suggestion, Vince became involved with Alateen, a group of teenagers whose lives were being adversely affected because of their own or another family member's abuse of alcohol. Eventually Vince's mother was persuaded to attend Al-Anon meetings to help her learn to live with an alcoholic.

Mr. Rudolph explained that alcohol addiction is the problem of the person who drinks. Some alcoholics recover; others do not. Meantime, living with that drinker or deciding to leave him or her is the concern facing other family members.

"Your responsibility, Vince, is to do the best job you can of preparing yourself to be an independent satisfied individual. That means graduating from high school, getting job training or going to college, keeping out of trouble, and getting a part-time job now if you can. A job would keep you away from home some of the time, too, which would be good for you and your parents. Don't throw yourself away simply because someone else in the family is doing just that."

WAS IT AS BAD AS YOU EXPECTED?

"I see you are with us, Perry," Miss Alvarez said the day after giving the assignment about confronting a family member with something unexpected. "Either you didn't carry out the assignment or you lived through it."

"Lived through it," Perry said. "When I tell you about it, you'll surely decide it's worth at least an A+."

"No doubt. What happened?"

Perry said, "You said something about startling our families, so I did. I told my parents I wanted a car."

Bart said, "What's so startling about that? A lot of kids have cars nowadays."

"That's what I told Mom and Dad," Perry said. "Only I said *most* kids."

"What was your parents' reaction?" Miss Alvarez asked.

"They laughed. The way you'd laugh if a five-year-old asked for a car."

"And?"

"Well, when I said that most kids my age have cars, they gave me a big fat lecture about how most kids get good grades. Most kids have jobs. Most kids are responsible and do their share of work around the house. Most kids have parents who aren't as hard up as we are. Most kids—"

"We get the picture," Roy said. "You're going to get the car, of course."

"As it happens, I might," Perry told him.

"That woke the sleepers, Perry," Miss Alvarez said. "And we really are interested in how you handled the dialogue."

Marcie added, "I am, anyway. If it worked for you, I might give it a try. I'm one of those poor kids who don't have cars."

Perry said, "I found out there's a difference between what parents *expect* and what they *want* of their kids. For instance, Mom and Dad expect me to act like a stupid kid, but they wish I'd act grown-up and responsible."

"So?" Richard prompted.

"So I decided that if getting a car means 'maturing,' as they call it, I'd mature. I said, 'You think I can't get good grades, don't you?' I didn't add that I also think I can't. I said, 'You want me to get a job. Why not?' I knew some reasons why not, but I didn't mention them. I said, 'You want me to work around home, so I'll work around home.' I didn't add that I don't want to work around home."

Roy interrupted. "Enough of what you said. What we want to know is what *they* said."

"Are you ready for this?" Perry asked. "After about an hour of haggling, they agreed that *if* I bring my grades up, *if* I get a job, *if* I work around home, *if* I start acting like a responsible teenager, they'll consider helping out with getting a car."

"Do you think you can do all that?" Linda asked.

"Maybe not, but it's something to work toward. A car's a pretty big motivation, you know."

"And even if you don't reach their standards and get the car, you'll be on the road toward that goal," Miss Alvarez pointed out. "Whatever happens, you can't be a complete loser unless you flub on all those expectations."

The class clapped, which was their way of saying they were plugging for Perry.

CHAPTER 7

Conflict Is a
Way of Life

An ideal time to discuss problem-solving came about naturally in Miss Alvarez's Family Living class one day when the teacher noticed that a student seemed to be unusually depressed.

"Colleen, is anything about our class bothering you?" Miss Alvarez asked. "New students sometimes have a left-out feeling, and since this is only your second week here..."

Colleen said, "It's not that. Everyone has been friendly and helpful. It's just that...Well, never mind."

The teacher nodded sympathetically. "If you'd rather not discuss it, we won't urge you to, but sometimes talking about problems helps."

"In this class we can talk about what's bugging us," Duane said.

"Sometimes we even figure out ways to deal with things," Marcie added.

"Like when I felt as if everyone was cutting me down," Perry said.

Colleen said, "I don't mind talking about my problem. It's just that no one can do anything about it."

"Let's talk about problems today," Miss Alvarez suggested. "There are ways of attacking them. Maybe as we talk you will decide which is the best plan for you, Colleen. But first, let's decide what problems are and who has them."

YOU'RE STANDING ON A STORY

"I know one thing," Roy commented, "living would be a lot easier if it weren't for problems."

"More comfortable," Miss Alvarez admitted. "However, is life without problems what we want? Think about a story or a movie you enjoyed. Then ask yourself these questions: Was there conflict? That is, were some characters in disagreement? Were characters linked together in some way, but not just right for each other? Was the main character faced with a difficult problem? Were there obstacles in the way of solving the dilemma?"

The students couldn't think of movies or stories that were without conflict.

"Why do authors write about people's problems?" the teacher asked.

"Otherwise the story would be boring," Duane answered.

Marcie said, "Also, our English teacher says we learn about life from reading how characters deal with troubles."

Miss Alvarez nodded. "That's exactly what makes a story. Someone has a problem to solve, but there are roadblocks. The character tries different ways to work things out but fails and has to start over with a different approach. Finally, the character either solves the dilemma or learns to adjust to it. The story pattern is attempt-fail, attempt-fail, and at last attempt-succeed."

Marcie added, "In English class we learned what you just said. Also, our teacher says some kind of change takes place in a story."

"Yes, and that word 'change' brings us to an important consideration in problem-solving," Miss Alvarez said. "If it weren't for problems, society wouldn't change and there would be no progress. Think about prehistoric people, for instance. They had to figure out ways to survive physically, and in doing so they made discoveries having to do with shelter, food, communication, and other innovations. Every generation contributes much in the way of inventions based on people's needs. All the time, too, we are discovering ways to be better parents and homemakers. Progress is the solving of problems."

"Okay, I'm convinced," Duane said, sighing.

Suspense is another important aspect of stories. It is created largely through characters' doing things that lead to disaster. As you read a book or watch a movie, you find yourself wanting to cry out to a character, "Don't do that! If you do, something terrible will happen." That same scenario is going on in your own life story. There are onlookers—parents and others—who feel they must warn you not to do certain things that spell trouble. Your response is that experience is the best teacher. That is true in many cases, but it doesn't have to be *your* experience. It can be that of someone who has traveled the road you are now on. That, of course, doesn't mean you can or should be shielded from all trouble and hardship. It means that your experience combined with that of certain other people equals wisdom.

In reading a story or watching a movie, you will note that people gouge one another with words as well as with weapons. You find yourself thinking, *Why did you say that? Didn't you know you were wiring yourself for a hurtful reply? You didn't have to tell him that! You can never erase something you have said.*

At many spots in the story tragedy might have been averted if only the characters had spoken and acted wisely and caringly. Likewise, there are many opportunities in our lives when different words or actions could point us in a smoother direction from the one we have chosen.

The most important element of a story is that the character must solve his or her own problem. In some cases, the situation can't be changed; it's a matter of learning to live gracefully with life the way it is rather than the way we wish it were.

What do we need to know if we are to deal with our own problems and help others with theirs?

WHAT CAUSES PROBLEMS?

Your needs began at the moment of conception and have been going on ever since. Because of those needs being met or not being met, you experience emotions, pleasant and unpleasant. The way feelings are expressed depends on your individual emotional pattern, which began with heredity. You have tendencies toward a certain temperament. In the light of that basic temperament, your emotional reactions are shaped through the process of learning and development. Environment plays a large role.

Your feelings cause you to behave in certain ways, and the people around you react to that behavior according to their emotional patterns. The clash of emotions resulting from people's needs bumping against one another creates many of our problems.

We are constantly trying to keep our lives in a state of balance, but things change, throwing our personal situations out of balance. Therefore, all of us have problems throughout life.

At first your problems were simple. All you had to fret about was being loved, nourished, and kept comfortable. But to the infant those needs are monumental. Their name is survival.

We might think of all behavior as an attempt to survive—not just to stay alive, but to be reasonably comfortable most of the time. Some behavior, such as breathing, is involuntary and some voluntary.

Behavior is our way of trying to get along in the world. It is an attempt to solve problems, but impulsive (thoughtless) behavior can create problems. For instance, we may say, "I couldn't help doing that," or "I got so mad I lost control." However, destruction of property and injury to others are behaviors that the individual decides to do or not to do. They are impulsive actions, but they are not involuntary.

KINDS OF PROBLEMS

Problems are of two types: developmental and special. *Developmental problems* occur at certain stages in a person's life and are typical of particular age groups. For instance, the child entering school is faced with adjusting to a new authority figure instead of parents. He or she also discovers that relating to a roomful of other children is different from being with brothers, sisters, and neighborhood playmates, or being an only child.

The teenage years present their typical problems of dating, graduating from high school, and trying to become independent of parents. Adult issues include marriage, children, career, aging, retirement.

In addition, each person has problems *special* to him or her. These might include ill health, physical or mental handicap, loss of loved ones, marital conflicts, employment troubles, or money worries, to name a few.

APPROACHES TO PROBLEMS

What about a situation that is severe enough to disrupt everyday functioning? There is probably no completely satisfying solution. You are faced with a few imperfect choices. If there were an ideal answer, there would be no problem.

A noted physician once explained the approach to problems somewhat as follows: Think of your problems as weeds that have taken over your yard. What can you do about those weeds? You can (1) get rid of them; (2) move somewhere else; or (3) learn to live with them.

What do weeds have to do with that course you are flunking, or the divorce your parents are getting, or the accident you had with the family car?

Direct Attack. Getting rid of the weeds means facing the problem head-on and solving it. This is sometimes referred to as "direct attack" or "direct approach." Such a method might work if you're failing a course, for example. The direct attack might be to study harder, to attend class more faithfully, to do extra assignments, to get a tutor, or to get help from teachers, parents, or other students. The best solution depends on the reason for the failure.

Avoidance. What about the moving-away-from-the-weeds approach? This plan, called "avoidance," can be either healthful or unhealthful. If the problem is a heart condition that is aggravated by high altitude, it makes sense to move to a lower elevation. If being with a certain person always winds up in a fight, the solution could be to avoid that person. If the problem is hating one's job, it might pay to get a different one.

On the other hand, avoidance can create an unhealthful attitude of running away from problems. Miss Alvarez asked her class to suggest kinds of unhealthful avoidance. The responses included suicide, hiding out from the law, running away from home, misuse of alcohol and other drugs, refusing to admit there is a problem, or doing nothing about it.

Acceptance. Learning to live with the weeds can be simply a matter of accepting them. The situation exists and cannot be corrected so the answer is to go ahead living as normally as possible.

Sometimes living with a problem can take the form of *substitution.* Since no direct solution is possible, we can work around the problem by settling for a partial solution. This is sometimes referred to as the "detour." Suppose a person's sight is permanently lost. The best solution would be to find ways of compensating for the loss, such as learning to read braille, developing a sensitivity to the differences in human voices, and perhaps relying on a guide dog. Blind people often become so successful in living without sight that others are unaware they can't see.

STEPS IN PROBLEM-SOLVING

You have a problem. (That's a safe guess.) Let's assume you have decided to approach your problem directly rather than to avoid it. But direct attack can be either healthful or unhealthful. A glance at a few newspaper headlines will reveal some destructive outcomes of attempts to deal with problems: "Jealous Husband Kills Wife and Lover." "Woman Found Guilty of Arson to Collect Insurance." "Fourteen-Year-Old Runs Away in Stolen Auto."

For your solution to be healthful, you need some *criteria* (measurements) to guide you. The decisions you make depend largely on your values and beliefs. If you are a caring person, you will want to work out your problem without unnecessary hurt to others. You will think of what is best for everyone involved, including yourself. But regardless of what philosophy is your guide, certain logical steps should be followed in the problem-solving process.

1. Define the problem clearly and specifically. You may have heard the saying, "You can't see the forest for the trees." That means you don't focus on the entire picture; you see only part of it. That can be a pitfall in problem-solving. You get hung up on one aspect rather than seeing the whole story. For instance, you may think a teacher is picking on you, and that appears to be the problem. The real issue, though, is the relationship between you and the teacher. Why are you and she or he in conflict? In any dilemma, be sure you know what the real problem is.

2. Collect data. Gather as much information relating to the problem as you can. Write the information down or talk about it with someone. Other people can't solve your problems, but talking a problem through helps to sort it out in your own mind.

In gathering information, there are two considerations— the rational (thoughtful) aspects and the emotional ones. The feeling part of us says, "I wish. . ." or "I want. . ." The thinking part says, "I should. . ." or "I must. . ." Our emotional side insists that the situation must turn out the way we desire, while our reason tells us it probably can't be just that way. During the process of examining the information, courses of action come to mind, and that leads into step 3.

3. Weigh the alternatives, listing the advantages, disadvantages, and probable outcomes of each. This process involves being considerate of yourself and others. State what the conflict is between your needs and those of someone else. The choice of action will be determined largely by your values and standards of behavior.

4. Decide which course of action to follow. Remember that it might fail. Your alternatives might need to be changed or revised later, but for now resolve to stick with your decision and give it your best effort.

5. Evaluate the results of your action from time to time. If it isn't working, try another plan.

WHAT CAN YOU DO WITH A PROBLEM?

The day after the discussion about problems, Colleen said she would like to talk in class about her situation.

"Perhaps we could help you work it through according to the steps we decided on," Miss Alvarez suggested. "How would you define your problem?"

"I wish I were still in Portland with my dad instead of here with my mother."

Miss Alvarez said, "Colleen has stated a problem. Let's list on the chalkboard some of the considerations, then center our discussion on them."

She listed the following questions:

1. Is Colleen's statement the real problem, or is it part of a larger one?
2. Can the problem be solved by the direct attack approach?

3. Who owns the problem?
4. What other people are involved?
5. What are Colleen's options?
6. What might be the outcomes of the various choices?

"Have I left out anything important?" the teacher asked.

"Deciding on the solution," Marcie suggested.

"I omitted that purposely. Do you know why?"

After a moment's thought, Marcie said, "Because Colleen has to make that decision. All we can do is help her think the problem through."

Miss Alvarez nodded. "Exactly. Colleen, would you like to describe your situation so we will have some information to base our discussion on?"

Colleen furnished the following information: She is an only child. Her parents are getting a divorce after twenty years of marriage. Colleen loves both of them and is deeply upset over the breakup of the family. The custody battle has not yet been settled. Meantime, Colleen was allowed to choose which parent to stay with. Part of her problem is not wanting to hurt either parent's feelings. When her mother moved to this town last summer to accept a job with the university, Colleen chose to remain in Portland with her father so that she wouldn't have to leave her friends or change schools.

Miss Alvarez said, "Let's stop and review the situation to this point. You couldn't solve the overall crisis of your parents' separation because that was their problem. So your immediate problem was choosing which parent to live with. Were there any other options?"

"I could have run away from home, but that wouldn't have solved anything," Colleen answered.

"So you decided on the direct attack approach. But

apparently that didn't work or you wouldn't be here now."

Colleen went on to explain that because of her anger, frustration, and feeling of loss, she had started skipping school and running around with some kids who were in trouble with the law. "Maybe I was trying to get even with my folks," she said, "but I'm the one who got hurt."

"And your mother and father, too, of course," Miss Alvarez reminded her.

"Sure. All of us. Anyway, my parents decided I'd have to come here and be with Mom until school's out. She can supervise me better than Dad can because he travels on his job."

"So you ran out of choices," Marcie summed up. "Where does that put you now?"

The class agreed that Colleen's choices were limited. Colleen admitted she was sometimes tempted to run away. The class talked about the new problems that alternative would create.

Colleen said, "Actually, I was trying to run away from the problem by getting into trouble instead of adjusting."

"Instead of living with the weeds," Evelyn added.

"So that means I'm stuck right here with Mom," Colleen finally decided.

"That brings us to the original approaches to problem-solving," Miss Alvarez said. "You can't kill the weeds. The problem, divorce, is there, and it isn't in your power to eliminate it. You have decided not to run away from the weeds; there would be a new crop wherever you went. What does that leave?"

"Just what Evelyn said. Learn to live with the weeds. I think maybe I can handle that better since we've talked about it. At least I know the people in this class care about me."

Perry said, "So even if you had to leave your friends in Portland, you've found some new ones here."

"And I won't make the same mistakes here that I did there. Since we've talked about it, I don't feel as if I have to get even with anyone anymore."

Miss Alvarez said, "Colleen, we have learned something important about you during this discussion."

Colleen looked surprised. "What's that?"

"You remember we said earlier that the way we approach problems depends largely on our values? Well, we learned that you have decent standards of behavior, so you weren't satisfied with the way you were acting in Portland. That you believe in facing problems directly rather than avoiding them. That you have consideration for the feelings of others. And, perhaps most useful of all, that you can learn from your mistakes and are willing to change. I also learned some things about the rest of you. You are loving, caring people. I feel as if I could trust you with my emotions in a crisis," Miss Alvarez told the class.

CHAPTER ◇ 8

Who Is It you
Want Me to Be?

S ometimes as adults we must learn how to do a better job of living because of unhealthy experiences during our growing-up years. Support groups can be useful in helping to erase the scars of an unhappy childhood. Members of one such group were invited to share parental sayings they had heard over and over again throughout childhood or teen years. Among the responses were:

This punishment hurts me more than it does you.
Respect your elders.
Mark my words.
Wait till I tell your father.
What will the neighbors think?
Just wait till *you* have kids!
Because I said so, that's why.
If I've told you once, I've told you a thousand times.
You're not the only pebble on the beach.

When are you going to start growing up?
Where did we go wrong?
After all I've done for you!
Be careful.
You're not old enough yet.
When *I* was your age. . . .
Who do you think you are?

You can probably add a few tattered bits of advice from your own family scene.

Let's analyze the reasons for parents' use of such overused phrases. What is a parent's greatest need? Generally speaking, to be a good parent, of course. Being responsible for the life of another human being is the most delicate and demanding job there can be. No wonder the parent is fearful that something will happen to destroy that brandnew person from the moment it is born through all the years of its life.

But why the repeated phrases in addition to hundreds of fresh ones? They are the parent's way of saying, *"Please* take care of yourself. You are my most precious creation; you are a part of me."

What do some of the phrases actually say? Take, for example, "This punishment hurts me more than it does you." That might be reworded to say, "I love you so much that I hurt when you hurt." "Respect your elders" means, "Please take me seriously; I must be in charge for at least a few more years." "Mark my words" implies that the parent is wiser than the child because of having lived longer; therefore if the child listens he or she may be saved some of the agony of life. "You're not the only pebble on the beach" means that I, the parent, also have needs and frustrations; I count, too. The two simple words, "Be careful," encompass all the hopes and fears of the parent. Don't be involved in an auto or motorcycle accident. Don't destroy your brain with drugs. Don't become a slave to alcohol, gambling, or other addiction. Don't leap into adulthood too soon by becoming a teenage parent before you have learned to be a teenage kid. Stay in school until you have earned a dipploma, which is your passport into a world that can be brutal, especially to the uneducated and the unskilled. Avoid situations that will lead you into danger and trouble. Obey the law; its purpose is to protect you. Stay well. Be happy. Be safe. Be loving. And please let me be your parent!

SOME MESSAGES HURT

Not all parental messages are loving ones. Through actions, if not words, a parent may tell a child: I didn't want you in the first place; I don't want you now. You are a burden and an interference in my life. You don't live up to my expectations. I would like to be rid of you. I don't want to deal with a handicapped child. Thank heaven my other kids aren't like you.

Hate messages of that sort are destroyers. They can create the monsters who inhabit our prisons and the distorted beings who require years of therapy and psychiatric attention. Some victims of hating parents never become well.

Most parents, though, love their children and strive to be good caretakers. In spite of good intentions, parents can damage their children through expectations that don't fit properly.

LIFE-STYLE? WHAT'S THAT?

Most of us probably think of life-style as standard of living—income, jobs, careers; where we live, what kind of neighborhood; what sort of home—how many bathrooms and TV sets; how many cars; membership in what groups; travel and leisure activities; education; educational levels of family members. In other words, we think of life-style as having to do with material possessions and social status.

Human behaviorists, on the other hand, define life-style as a family's values and beliefs and how the members ordinarily behave in various situations. Avoiding problems may be life-style for one person, whereas meeting life head-on may be another's mode of living. One person may go through life trying to get as much as possible for nothing, while another believes people should earn their way, working for all they get.

Members of the support group mentioned earlier talked about their childhood and teen experiences. Do you recognize your family pattern in any of the descriptions?

YOU'RE ON YOUR OWN, KID

Collin M. was an only child raised by his father following the death of Collin's mother when the boy was four. Mr. M. was a shift boss for a coal mine, which meant he worked sometimes at night, sometimes during the day, often at irregular times. He admitted that he didn't know how to discipline his son, and he was seldom around when the boy was in trouble or in need of adult direction. From early childhood on, Collin did pretty much as he liked. Desiring to be a good father, but not knowing what else to do, Mr. M. gave Collin whatever he wanted, including a motorcycle at an early age and an automobile before driving age. Nothing was expected of Collin in return. When he got in trouble for nonattendance at school, his father covered for him, saying he was ill or out of town. When Collin's motorbike got totaled, Mr. M. bought him another. When the boy was cited for driving a car without a license, his father cautioned him to be careful not to get caught the next time.

In talking with a school counselor, Collin admitted to a feeling of emptiness in his life. "You'd think it'd be a piece of cake having my own way about everything," he said, "but a lot of the time I can't get anyone to go along with me because other kids have rules. I think I'd have an easier time if there was someone to tell me what to do. Besides, I'm always in trouble with someone—neighbors, the school, the police, even my buddies. It burns them that I can do what I want and they can't."

"Do you think they would trade places with you?" the counselor asked.

Collin shook his head. "I think they feel a kind of safety even when they're wishing their own parents would bug off."

SHAPE UP!

Mel's complaint was the opposite of Collin's. "I felt as if I was living under a giant microscope," he said. "The worst of it was, Dad was determined to be a perfect father, and the only way he could do that was to have perfect kids. His motto could be, 'Whatever you're doing, stop it and do something else.'"

Mel's family was run rigidly on schedule. There were long lists of rules for each member (wife Elda, daughter Samantha, son Mel.)

"It was like punching a time clock for meals, homework, dressing and bathing, household chores—you name it," Mel said. "But the worst was that the rules kept changing. One week we could go to bed at eleven, and the next week at ten. Then there were new rules all the time. All at once, we couldn't have company on Sunday or holidays.

What was Elda's reaction to this dictatorship? She defied her husband by indulging Mel and Samantha. The more she did that, the more her husband expected of the children. Elda confessed to a marriage counselor that her husband felt so insecure about himself that he had to exert power over someone. "If it weren't for the children, I would have left him," she said. "But he would demand custody of the kids, and he would probably get it because he came across as a concerned father, whereas I might be portrayed as an indifferent permissive mother."

BEING THE AGE YOU ARE

You have probably been told at times to "act your age." Acting our age is necessary to good physical and mental health. According to the life cycle, we go through stages—infancy, childhood, adolescence, adulthood, old age—each characterized by certain expected behaviors.

Some children are pushed swiftly and dangerously through childhood by parents or society. Some plunge into marriage or parenthood before they have a chance to be teenagers.

James Hymes in his book *A Child Development Point of View* writes that the big task of parenting is "to let a child be a child."

Child behavior expert David Elkins describes "hurried children" as those who are expected to "take on the physical, psychological, and social trappings of adulthood before they are prepared to deal with them."

THE PROGRAMMED CHILD

Mr. and Mrs. K. are the brilliant parents of twelve-year-old Tracy, who inherited their superior intelligence. From

Tracy's infancy, Mr. K.'s goal has been to give his daughter every advantage to develop her mind and body, and Mrs. K. has gone along with that endeavor: Swimming lessons and exercise classes during babyhood. Stimulation gadgets and educational toys appropriate at each age level. Enrollment in preschool programs for developing creativity. A wide range of experiences, involving considerable travel. Mr. K. spoke to his daughter in several languages other than his own, beginning at birth; he believes this facilitated Tracy's learning of French and Russian along with English during early childhood.

This immense ambition to nurture a super child may have resulted in part from Mr. K.'s desire to make up for major disappointments from his college years. He had dreamed of being on the university football team, looking forward to being a well-known athlete and at the same time a superior scholar. However, he barely missed being chosen for the team, which to his mind spelled failure. An even greater blow to his ego occurred when he failed to earn a doctor's degree at the university when he felt that he genuinely deserved it.

As a parent, Mr. K. felt deeply gratified to have a superior daughter to achieve honors for the family. At the age of ten Tracy was entered in a gymnastics program with a view to becoming an Olympics contender as a teenager. She had already spent her early childhood being coached in a variety of sports, including golf, tennis, swimming, and gymnastics, along with tutoring in college preparatory subjects. Until she was twelve, Tracy was enrolled in private schools for the gifted.

Suddenly that year, to the shock of her parents, Tracy decided she wanted to attend a middle school in her own town. "After all the money and effort we've spent to make your life something special, why would you want to settle for a mediocre education in the public school system?" her parents wanted to know.

Tracy didn't attempt to explain. She couldn't understand it herself except to feel that something was missing in her life. It was as if she had never been a child making mistakes, getting into trouble, lying in the grass wasting time and watching clouds scudding across the sky. She'd never even had a friend to hang around with. Of course, there had been other children in her life, but they were all super kids like herself trying to beat everyone else's records.

Once she had determined to attend public school in a regular grade and had finally worn her parents down to allowing her to try it for a year, Tracy was filled with misgivings. When had she ever made a decision all on her own? And what if she blew it?

At first the year was a failure. Not academically; Tracy's grades were superior in all subjects. Sometimes the school work was downright boring; eighth-grade math, for instance, was almost absurd to a girl who had taken courses in college calculus. Then there was the matter of sports. Tracy, the athletic wonder, had problems with, of all things, volleyball! It wasn't that she lacked the skill to learn the game. The problem was her very superiority. She had never learned about teamwork in sports. Her competition had always been on an individual basis. Now she found herself becoming impatient with her teammates—with the foolish things they kept doing. Every time her team lost a game, she felt as if she personally had failed. Dealing with failure was not one of Tracy's skills.

Then there were peer relationships. This was Tracy's first experience in mixing with a cross section of humanity with its countless differences in economic level, social graces, language, dress, manners, and behavior. Although the students did not openly reject her, they didn't include her in their mischievous attempts to break free from the adult world and prove how grown-up they were. Tracy told herself it didn't matter since she was the most grown-up person in the school anyway. Sometimes she overheard their gossiping and felt a little secret desire to join in.

Sensing her discomfort, Tracy's parents promised to enroll her in a private school the following autumn. "You don't have to put up with that kind of treatment," they told her. "Who do those kids think they are, anyway?"

Thinking about that, Tracy decided her parents' message was, "We'll make the world right for you. You don't ever have to suffer."

Even as an overprotected twelve-year-old, Tracy sensed something wrong with that. "I don't want to be in a private school," she informed her parents. "I want to be like other kids. I'm going to make these kids like me or else!"

Tracy told the support group that was the wisest decision she ever made. "If there's one thing each of us has to learn," she said, "it's that managing the world is up to us. No one else can do it for you."

A SECOND CHANCE?

Probably everyone looks back on his or her past life with regrets and disappointment. Why did I waste all those years? Why did I get involved with that gang? Why didn't I listen to my parents? Why didn't I take school seriously? Why didn't I develop that talent? Why? Why? Why?

Often parents can't resist the temptation to relive their wasted youth through their children. Not only will they be making up to themselves for lost dreams, they reason, but they will be doing their children a favor by encouraging them to enrich their own lives.

Grady, another member of the support group, said that his father, Thad, a college basketball hero, had missed becoming a professional athlete. A piece of his ego had been stinging ever since. As a parent, Thad felt that a part of that hurt could be erased by following his son's athletic career through high school and college. Even if Grady never became a pro, think of the glorious years of watching him be an athletic star at school!

Thad's fervor began during Grady's childhood with Little League. Grady's enthusiasm was less than his father's. He got tired of having his father race out onto the field to argue with the umpires. He wanted to be fishing and collecting rocks in his spare time. During junior high and high school he resented the hours of practicing for sports that he wasn't exceptionally good at. The tales he heard about football camp terrified him, although he wouldn't have dared voice his misgivings to his fearless, athletic father.

In talking about his youth, Grady said his teen years were miserable because of a feeling of guilt about not living up to his father's expectations. "Except for that," he said, "I had an ideal family life. Comfortable standard of living. Good parents. Average grades. Plenty of friends. Normal activities except for the constant hassle over athletics. I realize now that I should have been more assertive and less guilt-ridden. That helps me in handling my own kids. I don't hesitate to make suggestions, but my hopes for them mustn't be in conflict with their desires about what to do with their lives."

Another group member, Ray, who sings with a country-western band in Nashville, says he would not trade his job and his life for any other. "I was born with musical talent," he explained, "and my mother had her heart set on my becoming a concert violinist. I knew that didn't figure in my plans, but I also knew I wouldn't be happy if I weren't using my giftedness in some way. That's where the band comes in. I love this music and this life. The ideal way to handle a family conflict over what you should do with your life is to arrive at some sort of compromise with your parents."

WHY CAN'T YOU BE LIKE YOUR SISTER?

A common difficulty in the job of parenting is the differences among the children in the family. It isn't unusual to hear a comment such as, "We never had a minute's problem with little Genevieve. Why can't our other kids be like her?" Chances are they had several minutes' difficulty with little Genevieve, but right now little Buddy's problems are blotting out some of those memories.

"How can Harry and I be the parents of four kids so different from one another?" Shirley Knox wonders. "After all, we did raise them the same way."

When questioned about the differences, Shirley described her children: "Well, there's Luke, our firstborn. He's bright and friendly, a real go-getter. Vivian, on the other hand, is moody, slow to respond to people. I swear she's been temperamental since the day she was born. Bernice is the predictable one. Easygoing, takes everything in stride. An easy child to manage. Then there's Skeeter!" Shirley sighed and gave a little laugh. "There's no keeping up with that one. Life is one big circus for Skeeter. I think he was born laughing, and he hasn't taken anything seriously during the seven years since."

What Shirley says about her children is, in effect, what

research is finding to be true. *Constitutional makeup*—the physical and mental qualities one is born with—has an influence on personality. At least part of your future was determined before you came into the world.

Parents react to the inborn qualities, and their reactions can reinforce the tendencies. Thus, a child's personality is affected very early in life by parental reactions to the child's moods.

For instance, Mr. and Mrs. Knox may have been so overwhelmed by overactive Skeeter that they responded with impatience. Skeeter may unconsciously interpret their irritation as a sign that they don't like him. Since Bernice is an easy child to manage, she receives less of her parents' time and attention. She might suspect that her parents are more interested in her siblings than in her.

Children who have the perception of not being liked by parents or other key persons in their lives often react to the hurt by misbehaving. The more troublesome the child's actions, the more annoyed and critical the parents become. Punishing the child is then likely to deepen her or his hurt and anger, causing even more unacceptable behavior.

Misbehavior can also result from a situation like Bernice's. If she feels ignored, she may imitate her brother Skeeter to gain parental attention. Or perhaps she may become withdrawn to an unhealthy degree since people expect her to be quiet and undemanding.

WHO'S IN CONTROL?

Why do parents act like parents? A degree of power is a major need throughout life. Parents want to have a feeling of being in control of their own destiny. A lack of control over their lives often causes them to act in destructive ways.

Why do kids act like kids? They fear losing control in their relationships with parents. Teens are frightened that they are being treated like children and thus losing control of their lives. To assert their rights, they may behave in ways that worry their parents.

It is important for a person to grow up with feelings both of having control and of being controlled. Parents are in a position to help shape children's lives. No one is absolutely free to run his or her own life all the time. Learning to accept control is important to getting along with others and living in society. But it is also important for everyone to have choices. Among the choices of the teenager is planning what to do with the future.

DO MY PARENTS REALLY LOVE ME?

If you feel that your parents treat you unfairly or care less about you than about your siblings, by all means talk about it with them. They don't see themselves the way you see them. Also, you don't see yourself exactly as you are. Not only do we need mirrors to see how we look physically; we need mirrors for viewing our personalities. Those mirrors are the people in our lives.

If your hair is sticking out all over the place, you can comb it. If your faults are sticking out all over the place, you can rearrange those, too. You belong to you.

It's not only who *you* think you are that counts; it's also important who others think you are.

CHAPTER ◇ 9

Your Spot in the
Family Portrait

What family members expect of one another depends on many conditions. Some you can control; some you can't. For instance, you can't decide where or when to be born. You have no choice as to race or nationality. You can't choose your heredity. You can't exchange your parents, your siblings, or your other relatives. You can't choose your birth order in the family; you are stuck with being the oldest, youngest, only, or in-between child.

What does that leave? Family patterns tend to be passed along from generation to generation. Your family's life-style is built into the fabric of your personality from infancy. Wealth and ambition are likely to be passed from parents to children. So are poverty, battering, child abuse, alcoholism and other drug dependencies, dropping out of school, and unemployment. Does that mean that we are trapped in our family's destiny?

"Coping with" does not necessarily mean putting up

with. It often means bringing about change. As the students in Miss Alvarez's Family Living class learned, your life is a story. Any good story has conflict and some kind of change taking place.

TURNING POINT

Carmen, the mother of teenage Manuel and Carmelita, came to this country after a shabby childhood and youth in Puerto Rico. By age sixteen she had been married briefly and given birth to two children. The children were taken from her by relatives, who decided that Carmen was an unfit mother. In the meantime, Carmen's husband abandoned her. She then teamed up with a young man she met at a street dance and came to the United States with him. She believes he is probably the father of Manuel and Carmelita. Carmen has lived with several men, all of whom disappeared sooner or later. She has learned to expect nothing from life except bad luck. Life is a series of episodes, usually with a temporary partner. She doesn't expect anything to last. So what if your children are snatched from you and your "husbands" vanish? Carmen takes that kind of thing for granted. Everything bad ends sometime, she reasons. So does everything good, like a job. Since she expects nothing good to happen, she is seldom disappointed.

When asked what she wants for her children, Carmen says Carmelita will probably get married and have a "bunch of kids." Manuel is a different story, though. Carmen wishes he would go to school, but she expects that he will stay with the street gang and probably get killed or wind up in prison.

Carmen assumes that the family will always be on welfare, but the "kids" are expected to show up with food and money from time to time. Carmen doesn't try to find out where the handouts come from.

Manuel describes life as a "bummer." "You're either a 'have got' or a 'haven't got,'" he says, "and we're 'haven't gots.' As for the gang, that's exciting, a real challenge. So what if you get wasted? What's the point in staying alive anyway? You get more attention when you're dead. One dreamer in the family's enough. That's my sister. If she wants to go through life in a bubble, who am I to haul her back down to earth?"

Carmelita, the "dreamer," has a different philosophy. "No way am I going through life sharing my house with cockroaches and rats!" she says. "I've had it with broken toilets, rusted pipes, and peeling walls. And I'm not about to be owned by welfare. I don't know why I was put on this earth, and I don't know how long I'll be here, but I do know part of the world belongs to me and I'm going to manage it my own way."

Carmelita's "own way" is to go to school every day and to learn everything she can. Schoolwork is not easy for her. She has grown up without books, magazines, or television. Her language is a mixture of Spanish, English, profanity, and bad grammar. "But somehow I have to climb out of this trap I'm in," she insists. "That means working at it every minute. When Manuel and I were little kids, Mom taught us to shoplift. I thought that was how everyone got along. That fell apart one day when I was caught with a sack of groceries while I was sneaking out of the supermarket. The store manager zeroed in on me, and then the police came. Naturally I was scared to death, not so much of the police as of what Mom would do when she found out I'd failed. Actually, that was a turning point in our life. We got referred to social services, which is a polite term for welfare." Carmelita laughed when she said that.

"Social services tries to supervise our family—give us food stamps, encourage Mom and Manuel to find jobs, things like that. But Mom and Manuel aren't about to pick up any new habits. They like things the way they are."

Carmelita does not like her family the way it is, but she knows she can be responsible for only one person—herself. The place she likes best is the school with its smell of chalk dust and cleaning compounds. While other students are scrambling to get out of the building at the end of the school day, Carmelita is staking out hiding places where she can spend the night without being spotted by the custodians. One of her worst moments came when she was found hiding behind some large plants in the biology lab. She didn't admit spending nights in the school, but she told the custodian that she liked to be there rather than go home to her shabby house. As a result, she was given an after-school job as a janitorial assistant.

She was also referred to the school counselor, to whom she admitted her home situation. Mrs. Lawton, the counselor, said, "No one would suspect that you live like that. You are always clean and neat."

Carmelita said, "That's because I take phys. ed. I can have a shower every day. And now that I have the job here at school, I can buy a few clothes and some material to make stuff in sewing class. Of course, Mom expects me to give her most of the money I make."

"We can fix that," Mrs. Lawton said. "I'll get you into a bookkeeping class so you can learn how to open a savings account where your money will be safe. Also, the school has a work program, so that you can be trained for a summer job. Meantime, we can add your name to the list of students who baby-sit. That way you can be away from home some evenings and weekends while you are earning money."

For Carmelita a new life had begun. "Best of all," she said, "I've discovered that there are people who want to help if you are willing to share your problems with them."

THE FAMILY LIFE CYCLE

Families differ just as individuals do, but most families go through a series of stages, each with its own kind of problems. Typically, the stages are marriage, parenthood (for some), middle age, old age. During each stage family members interact with one another, causing the entire family to be in a constant state of change and adaptation. Expectations change as roles change. For instance, each member of a marriage must exchange the major role of son or daughter for that of husband or wife. Even before that role begins to fit comfortably, the individual may find himself or herself having to start acting like a parent. The parent role usually lasts for many years and is difficult to discard when sons and daughters decide to run their own lives. The role of old age is healthy and fulfilling for many, but for some it is a time of illness, loneliness, or boredom. Most difficult of all, some old people become dependent on others to take care of them. This is devastating for someone who has spent much of a lifetime caring for others.

IT'S BECAUSE OF WHEN YOU WERE BORN

It's not enough that you have to switch roles several times during your lifetime. You may also be assigned certain roles according to your place in the birth order. Psychologists believe that birth order can have an effect on personality.

Children express their feelings about what is expected of them: "I'm sick of being referred to as 'the little mother' just because I have to take care of my kid sisters and brother while Mom works." "Being the oldest means being the good example in our family." "Being an only child has its advantages, but it's awful having your parents hovering over you all the time." "Being in the middle is like being erased. My parents spend so much time worrying that Lon, the oldest, will get into trouble, and so much time playing with Moe, the baby, that Jody and I are ignored half the time." "Being the oldest can be a pain, but on the other hand it means more privileges as well as more responsibility."

According to Dr. Louise Forer, a psychologist specializing in birth order, the oldest child in the family is likely to feel a more-than-ordinary need to please others. The middle child goes through childhood with knowledge that there's someone older, wiser, and more skilled. This may cause him or her to develop the ability to compromise in order to get along with parents and others.

Some experts suggest that the "baby" of the family runs the risk of being spoiled by too much attention, or of being ignored or put down by older siblings.

The important thing about birth order is not to take it too seriously. It may help you to understand why you and your siblings are expected to conform to assigned roles. Then you can decide whether or not the roles are appropriate. If not, talk it over with the family and decide if there is need for some changes.

THIS ISN'T THE FAMILY I ORDERED

The breaking up of families is a major cause of role change.

When Mr. V. died, his widow began to rely heavily on her son, Harvey, not only to carry on the tasks commonly thought of as "men's work," but also for comfort and counseling. "I felt as if I were expected to act like a husband instead of a son," Harvey complained. "Mom expected me to spend hours with her talking about business affairs and her feelings. I realized it was up to me to take on a lot more responsibility, but I just didn't feel like a teenager anymore."

The term "broken family" has a negative ring because it usually represents loss, and it always involves adjustment and change in roles. But a broken family need not spell disaster, and change can be either favorable or unfavorable. The world is changing continually, and so are we. No group of two or more persons remains the same in membership forever. However, divorce, remarriage, adoption, death, or any other irregularity in the typical family pattern calls for stressful adjustments.

Many families function more happily after a breakup than before. This is reflected in the comments of some teenagers:

"I went through childhood fatherless and wishing for someone besides my mom to tell me what to do. Now when my new stepfather cracks down on me pretty hard, I take it to mean he cares about me. It feels great!"

"Having my father die was the worst thing that ever happened to me. Mom and I went through a long time of grieving, but it brought us closer together than we had ever been. Now that we are getting back to normal, we have some fun times together."

"It sounds silly to say that divorce brought peace to our family, but that's what happened. Not only did our parents quarrel all the time, but my sister and I fought constantly, sometimes actually hurting each other physically. We were a family of nervous wrecks, and all of us blamed each other. Then Mom and Dad got a divorce with joint custody. Each of us girls spends every other month with one parent. You can't believe what good friends Sis and I have become. For that matter, Mom and Dad are almost like friends now. Each parent has one kid, and each kid has one parent, all the time."

"It's great having a stepbrother after being an only child. Now there's someone in the family to talk to and do things with besides just my dad. He and my stepmother have so many problems to work out that they aren't breathing on us all the time."

CHAPTER 10

Who's in Control:

Your Emotions

or You?

E motions play an immense role in what people expect of one another, and also in how we react to those expectations. We expect something because of feelings or desires. We respond to expectations depending on how we feel about them.

OTHER PEOPLE HAVE FEELINGS, TOO

Alan spent the school day in a state of anxiety. It began first period in art class when Mr. Macy yelled, "Okay, Alan, I'll see you after school."

"How come?" Alan wanted to know.

"I've had it with your fooling around in here. Just settle down now and we'll discuss the problem at three-thirty."

Alan's first reaction was one of bewilderment. Sure, he

had been clowning around when the bell rang, but how was that different from other days? Mr. Macy was an easygoing teacher. What had caused him to flare up this morning?

Once Alan recovered from his shock, other emotions began crowding in. First, he felt angry. Why did the teacher pick on him when other kids were also acting up? Along with the anger was a feeling of hurt. Alan had thought Mr. Macy liked him and enjoyed having him in class. Now he wasn't so sure. The hurt made Alan feel vengeful; he had a desire to get even. Remembering the scene, Alan was also embarrassed. Why had Mr. Macy bawled him out in front of the class?

Thinking about that made Alan angry all over again. Besides all those feelings, there was a measure of fear. Alan found himself dreading the after-school session. What if Mr. Macy told his parents he had misbehaved? They would probably ground him for the rest of his life, or at least until after Homecoming. Among the major expectations of Alan's family were decent grades and getting along with people in authority, including teachers.

Suppose Mr. Macy informed the vice principal about Alan's misbehavior. That might even mean suspension from school. Or Mr. Macy might decide not to let Alan go on the Art Club trip.

By the time school was over, Alan's emotions seemed to be one giant tangle in the middle of his stomach. However, the meeting with Mr. Macy turned out to be not so bad after all. The teacher opened the conversation by saying, "Sorry I yelled at you this morning, Alan. I could have handled things in a better way."

"It wasn't like you to zoom in on me like that," Alan said. "Took me off-balance."

"Maybe I'm not myself this week," Mr. Macy admitted.

"Did you know that a box of T-shirts the Art Club is selling was stolen during the game Saturday night?"

"Wow! No wonder you were upset. I guess my fooling around didn't help matters."

The teacher nodded. "Most mornings you kids take longer than you should to settle down to work, but ordinarily it doesn't bother me enough to make an issue of it. Today I was already on edge, so the first person I noticed wasting time lighted my fuse, and that happened to be you. I should have gotten after all of you sooner about this before it got out of hand."

Alan said, "And we kids should have realized you weren't going to put up with our funny stuff forever."

WHAT YOU SHOULD KNOW ABOUT EMOTIONS

What did Alan learn about emotions that might be useful to us? He found out that a person is likely to experience more than one feeling at a time. It is difficult to tell which emotion is the strongest. Alan was feeling puzzled, angry, embarrassed, hurt, vengeful, and fearful all at the same time. Sometimes a person may have emotions that contradict each other. A girl might be in love with a boy, yet hate him for preferring another girl. We might admire someone at the same time that we are envious of him or her.

The conference with Mr. Macy was important because it made Alan realize that emotional reactions depend a great deal on how a person is feeling. Alan was able to look at the art class crisis in a reasonable way when he learned his teacher's feelings and reasons for being angry. He was relieved to be able to let Mr. Macy known how he felt. In discussing the issue, both Alan and his teacher assumed some of the blame for the blowup. As a result, both will probably have better control over their behavior in similar situations.

When parents' expectations seem unreasonable, you become swept up in your own feelings, forgetting that your parents are acting the way they are on account of *their* feelings.

Facing the person or persons involved in a disturbing situation is important in dealing with emotions. Alan was tempted not to meet Mr. Macy after school. Not facing up to unpleasant feelings is called "avoidance."

Avoidance, both physical and emotional, can be either healthy or damaging. If we see a tornado coming, it makes sense to seek shelter below ground. Sometimes we must experience hurt in order to be healthy. The discomfort of a shot of Novocain is preferable to the pain of having a tooth drilled. The same is true of emotional hurts. It may be sensible to stay away from people we can't get along with, for instance, but not dealing with unpleasant incidents as they arise only postpones the hurt. It is important to deal with feelings while they are still new, rather than storing them away. Emotions that are not expressed lodge inside a person as physical illness or emotional pain. They don't go away. Get in the habit of hanging a mental sign on your unpleasant emotions—"Danger—Do not store in a dark place!"

As a teenager expressed it, "Feelings are the same in all languages, and all tears are the same color."

Since emotions are constantly with us, telling us what to say and do, it is important to learn about them, so that we are in charge of our own behavior and understand why other people act in ways that bother us.

WHAT IS AN EMOTION?

What are emotions? Where are they? How did we get them? Emotions are feelings that may be either negative or positive. Negative ones make us feel bad, and positive ones make us feel good. Grief, anger, boredom, jealousy, loneliness, hate, worry, fear, and envy are unpleasant emotions. Joy, love, admiration, relief, happiness, serenity, and contentment are positive.

Emotions are not to be confused with physical sensations such as heat, cold, hunger, thirst, physical pain, and weariness. However, physical conditions have an effect on emotional states. It is easier to be cheerful when we are well than when we are sick. We are likely to feel depressed when we are tired, hungry, or run-down. Our glands influence our emotional states.

Although there is evidence that emotional states originate in the brain, the emotion itself isn't located in any specific area of the body, such as the heart. It is an overall feeling that results from a happening in a person's life. However, emotions have so great an effect on the body that sometimes we actually feel those changes in specific spots—head, stomach, or neck, for instance.

Where do emotions come from? Are we born with them? When you were born, you cried. Were you angry? Sorrowful? No. You hadn't developed an emotional system yet. You cried to get necessary oxygen into your lungs. Later, during those early months of life, you cried to express physical discomfort—a stomachache, a pricking pin, an insect bite. As you grew older, your crying was still an expression of physical discomfort. But besides that, you learned to cry to express emotion—grief, anger, joy, sympathy, worry, fear, relief, disappointment, jealousy.

So most emotions are learned, not inborn, although our

brain chemistry does have an effect on our emotional makeup. At birth the baby's only expression of emotion is a state of excitement displayed by thrashing movements of arms and legs. Some scientists say we are born with basic fears of loud noises and of falling. Other authorities say those are not fears, but startle reactions; in other words, the new baby is startled by loud noises or loss of support.

Although we are not born with emotions, we do inherit certain temperamental tendencies. Emotions are part of personality. We sometimes characterize people by describing their emotional states. For instance:

Moody.
Cries at the drop of a hat.
Complaining, as usual.
Always looks on the bright side.
Gutsy.
An angry guy.

Some people, like Mr. Macy, go through life in a generally calm, easygoing fashion, while others are excitable by nature. We speak of the Mr. Macy type as being "low-key," while certain others impress us as being "hyper" or "highstrung." Emotional pattern is a significant aspect of personality. Added to that basic pattern are other emotions, some developed at given ages, some learned.

Developmental emotions show up as the person matures. They occur at certain stages without being taught. For instance, babies begin to express some happiness at about three months. By five months, children begin to show signs of anger, fear, and disgust. Now that cry may say, "I'm mad! Hurry up and feed me!"

By the age of two the development of basic emotional patterns is complete. Children have learned to express feelings. They have discovered that some behaviors work and some don't. Maybe that temper tantrum doesn't get people's attention anymore.

How do we know that emotional patterns are developmental? Since learning takes place largely through imitation, you would think that children who cannot see or cannot hear would not pick up fear, anger, joy, and other emotions because they can't observe the people around them. However, children who are deaf or blind, even from birth, show practically the same patterns of emotional behavior as others.

Although certain emotional states develop as the child matures, some specific emotions are learned. Love is developmental. At given ages the child who is loved develops affection for family members and then for other people. But he or she may learn from parents or others to love or hate a certain person or a racial, religious, or other ethnic group. Early in life, fear becomes a part of the child's emotional pattern. Throughout life, this takes the form of specific fears that are learned. We learn to be afraid of running into the street when there is traffic. We learn to be afraid of fire when we realize its dangers.

WHAT TRIGGERS THOSE FEELINGS?

An emotion is a reaction to what enters your mind. The five senses—sight, sound, taste, touch, and smell—are the gateways to the brain.

Emotions can be troublesome because they are for the most part involuntary, meaning they show up without our choosing. We don't just decide to be hurt over what someone said, to be scared of a vicious dog, or to be delighted by a compliment. We just are. Because an emotion appears without being invited, we are likely to respond without thinking. When we are hurt, our first reaction may be a desire to hurt someone else. Just as the emotion is involuntary, so might be the body's response to it. We can't stop certain physical reactions—that blush, those sweaty palms, the chattering teeth, the body's trembling.

It isn't always the way things are that brings an emotional response. It is often the way things *seem* to be. From his experience with Mr. Macy, Alan learned that one person's emotional outburst is likely to trigger an emotional reaction in someone else. What the reaction is depends on how the person perceives the situation. Alan perceived Mr. Macy as being unfair until they talked and Alan understood why Mr. Macy had turned his anger on him.

The feeling you have in connection with a certain happening may carry over into other similar experiences. For example, four-year-old Jonathan has been physically mistreated by his father. Even though his mother tries to reassure him that not all fathers are brutal, Jonathan is fearful when his mother remarries. It may take a long while for the stepfather to win Jonathan's trust.

BOXED-UP FEELINGS WANT TO BREAK FREE

It is normal to show how we feel. However, showing our feelings doesn't mean we are supposed to run around shrieking, crying, kicking, punching people, or screaming with laughter. It means being able to express feelings without damaging ourselves or others. On the other hand, have you ever heard someone called a "cold fish"? That cold fish probably has the same emotions bubbling around inside as you do but hasn't learned to let others know how he or she feels. In learning to deal with emotions, there are three major considerations: (1) the way you feel; (2) the effects on your body; and (3) the resulting behavior.

Behavior is the mirror that reflects feelings. Unacceptable behavior says a person is hurting. Emotions are so powerful a force in our lives that we tend to express our feelings in extreme terms: "Dad will kill me if I'm late." "I adore french fries." "I'll die if I don't pass that course."

We feel the way we do because our needs are, or are not, being met, and that is what makes an emotion important. You don't need to apologize for how you feel. In talking about what bothers them, teenagers often start by saying, "This probably isn't important. . ." However, if something seems important to you, it is. If it hurts, it's important.

EXPRESS OR CONTROL?

On one hand, we are told it is important to express emotions rather than store them. At the same time, we are told to learn to control our emotions. Doesn't that present a conflict?

Expressing feelings does not mean always letting them pour out in the way you would like, or at the time you would like. Handling of feelings in a healthy way requires a combination of "blowing off steam" in an emotional way and using reason and intelligence in deciding how to behave. You might be upset over a classroom incident, but after class might be a better time than during class to tell the teacher how you feel.

Are you upset about something? Of course; who isn't? Plan how to get your feelings out in the open with the least hurt to yourself and others. Looking ahead can prevent permanent scars.

Think of your emotions as if they were children. Consider what will happen if you box them away before they have expressed themselves. When sealed-in anger does break free and fly into action, it may hit innocent targets. Vandalism, rape, hijacking, and arson are examples of anger that breaks out of harness. Those are extreme cases, but the same thing happens on a milder scale time after time in our daily lives.

Suppose Clint Foye is working in his garden one evening. Clint's neighbor, Forrest Miller, comes over for a chat. There's no problem until Forrest says, "I see your son got his name in the paper."

Now Mr. Miller has hit a nerve. Emotions begin to simmer in Clint Foye. The first of these is annoyance. Why can't this jerk mind his own business? Who does he think he is to lord it over his neighbors?

Why is Mr. Foye's reaction a negative one? Because his son's name was in the newspaper for running a stop sign, resulting in an accident. To add to the aggravation, Mr. Miller's son's name had been in the paper the week before for being on the school's honor roll.

Now Mr. Foye's annoyance is gathering steam and taking the form of hatred for this overbearing neighbor and his honor-roll son. He is also feeling anger toward his own son for disgracing the family. He is experiencing some fear, too, fear that he is losing control of his boy. Then there's embarrassment over what people might be thinking.

How does Clint Foye handle his feelings? He laughs and tosses the situation off as unimportant. "Yeah, kids will be kids," he says. Does that take care of his negative feelings? No. Neither the laugh nor the remark expressed Mr. Foye's true emotions, so those feelings stay very much alive and full of energy.

Mr. Foye goes into the house with the intention of exploding at his son. Robert isn't around, though, so Mr.

Foye blows up at his wife. "You mean you let that kid leave the house after what happened yesterday?"

"I didn't let him. He just left," Lucy Foye says in a blaze of anger. "And you can quit yelling at me. Maybe if you'd discipline Robert once in a while..."

How does Mrs. Foye handle her emotions at that point? She rushes out of the room and slams the door.

It isn't until several days later that the Foye family are able to sit down and talk about their problems reasonably. Meantime, both Mr. and Mrs. Foye have taken out their irritability on each other and on other people, including their daughter.

When the Foyes finally decide a family conference is in order, they find out that Robert is going through a frustrating period of trying to outgrow his parents.

"You treat me as if I'm ten years old," he tells them.

"Maybe that's why he ran through the stop sign," his thirteen-year-old sister, Jan, suggests. "Maybe he's tired of being told what to do all the time, so he decided to get even with the law, as well as with you."

The family talk wasn't entirely calm and reasonable. Tempers flared, and hurtful things were said. In the long run, though, it was a healing experience. All four members were honest about how they felt and were willing to set up some rules that would define limits but at the same time allow more freedoms.

Might some of the family's rage have been drained off earlier to avoid some of the hurt? Perhaps Robert could have told his parents in words how he felt, rather than acting irresponsibly. Too often young people assume that their parents won't listen to them, so they let people know how they feel through angry behavior.

When Mr. Miller brought up an embarrassing subject,

Mr. Foye might have let Forrest know how he felt with a comment, "Of course we are upset about Robert's running the stop sign, but we do consider it a family matter that we will handle in our own way."

That would have told Mr. Miller tactfully that he was out of line and would have taken care of some of Mr. Foye's annoyance on the spot. Mrs. Foye might have said more to her husband about how she felt instead of walking out on the argument.

FRAGILE—HANDLE WITH CARE

Constant turmoil is a mark of an unhealthy family. In a healthy family members enjoy one another and are concerned with each one's welfare. However, even stable families represent a tangle of feelings, all interacting with one another. Each member is doubtless thinking at times, "No one understands how I feel!" And that can be true. Each person's own hurts and triumphs can be so overpowering as to blot out everyone else's. In a healthy family all members are aware that emotions are normal and must be expressed. Words are a powerful tool for keeping in touch with one another's feelings. When words fail, behavior takes over, sometimes with disastrous outcomes.

One of your difficult tasks is to accept the fact that much of the time family members don't suit one another. They often get on each other's nerves. And it's all because people keep acting like people.

Try to remember at all times that you are responsible for those feelings of yours that are constantly crying for attention. Listen to them; take charge of them; share them. Remember, too, that you hold other people's feelings in your hands. Don't crush, spindle, or mutilate. Handle feelings with care, no matter whose they are.

CHAPTER 11

Life Is Stress;

Stress Is Life

L et's shrug off today's annoyances and imagine ourselves back in prehistoric times. Our ancestor, Lod, is coming out of his cave and setting off for the day's work, which is to forage for food. Along the way he comes face to face with a threatening, unfamiliar beast. Lod has two choices. He can try to club the creature to death or he can turn and run like crazy. That is what psychologists now call the "fight or flight" reaction.

But who cares about Lod? Perry Grayling's present worry is that today he is supposed to take part in a panel discussion for English class. What's the problem? First, he turns to jelly at the very thought of appearing in front of a class. Second, he did not do his part of the research and isn't prepared. So what's another poor grade in that class? Plenty! This course is a graduation requirement. If he doesn't graduate, his parents will either die or kill him.

Meantime, he is not only letting himself down, but also his teacher and fellow panel members. Fight or flight?

Flight sounds good. Perry would love to leave town, but that isn't practical. His parents won't let him stay home from school, even if he says he's sick. In fact, he does feel sick at the thought of the upcoming assignment.

Fight? There's no one to fight with. At the moment, Perry would trade places with Lod and the wild beast.

What do Perry and Lod have in common besides the condition of being human? Not only is Perry experiencing stress, but so is practically everyone else. Even the babies being born at this moment are under stress. That's only the beginning, though. Stress will be showing up regularly in the life of each of those babies from now on. As long as you have to go through life with stress for a companion, you need to know enough about it to become its master.

STRESS: WHAT IS IT?

We usually think of stress as being an event or condition that is upsetting. From the medical-scientific standpoint, stress is something that triggers bodily reactions to unusual situations. Dr. Hans Selye, foremost pioneer and expert on this subject, defines stress as the "rate of wear and tear in the body." Perry Grayling says stress is "what happens to your body when something bugs you."

Stress is of two types—external and internal. External refers to conditions outside the body, such as war, earthquake, or divorce. Internal stress originates within ourselves. It may be an aspect of development, such as the chemical changes that take place in the body during adolescence. An external stressor can be identified as the cause of distress. Internal stress may take the form of depression or anxiety, a feeling of dread, threat, or fear when no definable danger is present.

STRESS: WHAT CAUSES IT?

Stress is the result of some sort of change. The change can be either pleasant or distressing. The amount and kind of stress we experience varies because it depends on many personal factors. The degree of stress you are subject to began with your heredity. Some of those thousands of genes you inherited point in the direction of excitability or calmness. That, in turn, has much to do with your physical and emotional reactions to stressful events. Then consider environment. From the moment of conception on, you are subject to a lifetime of stressful episodes. A horrifying example is the baby who is born to a drug-addicted mother and comes into the world also addicted.

Happenings awaken emotions—pleasant or unpleasant—that cause you to behave in certain ways. The combination of behavior and environmental impact creates problems. Your personality, which has been taking shape since your conception, determines how you deal with those problems. Part of your personality is how you perceive the world. Your perception of an event determines the amount of stress you experience from it. Perception has to do with needs. The more an incident interferes with your physical and psychological needs, the greater the stress.

Stress is involved, either pleasantly or unpleasantly, in human relationships, including family. Each change in the life cycle—birth, childhood, adolescence, dating, marriage, parenting, old age, and death—carries built-in stressors. And of course there are the countless unforeseens. Stress is so much a part of health that we have trouble deciding when it is the cause of health problems, and when the result.

STRESS AND THE ADOLESCENT

Someday, looking back on his adolescence, Perry may wonder how he could have been upset over something as minor as an English assignment. What is trivial to the adult, however, may be major to the child or adolescent. Students in a Denver high school listed the following as major causes of teen stress: parents' divorce, boyfriend/girlfriend conflicts, death in the family, school, alcohol and other drugs, peer pressure. They also mentioned changing schools, getting in trouble, and getting in fights. During the 1980s a survey of teenagers conducted from Vanderbilt University in Nashville found that the stresses most troubling to adolescents were failing grades, parental fighting, serious illness in the family, death in the family, and boy-girl breakups.

Why are the teen years a time of special anxiety? Stress is provoked by change and loss. Adolescence carries a large share of both: physical and chemical changes in the body; moving from junior high to high school; new teachers; new sets of classmates; separation from some friends; family changes as members marry or go away to school or jobs; finding it increasingly difficult to resist peer pressures because of a desire to "belong"; being forced to make choices—some healthy, some not; new and frightening expectations, including making post–high school plans, maintaining a decent grade-point average, competition in being accepted by a college of your choice (or your parents' choice), wondering what is expected of you by the opposite sex, wanting to be yourself and at the same time live up to the expectations of others.

Typical teen losses include saying good-bye to child-hood. Even though you rebel at being treated like a child, you can't help grieving now and again for the carefree time when your decisions were made for you and you were cared for and indulged. As you grow older, there are more losses of friends and family members who die, divorce, or move away. It is not unusual for a teenager to experience the loss of a classmate or relative through suicide or accident. Many teenagers suffer permanent physical or brain injury from accidents or drug abuse. Then there are the more everyday losses of not being a winner in athletic or scholastic competitions and countless other longings.

We perform and achieve largely because of what is expected of us. Stress can be the result of feeling that we can't live up to the many expectations of our society, parents, teachers, employers, peers, and selves. An expectation is too great to handle when it is in conflict with reality. Raymond, for instance, finds high school work difficult, yet his father expects him to go to college. In this case, the parental expectation is the *stressor* (the condition that causes stress). Children who feel they can't satisfy their parents are likely to grow up to be perfectionists who expect too much of themselves.

STRESS: DOES IT SERVE A PURPOSE?

In time of extreme stress, we feel that we are "falling apart" physically. Actually our bodies are "coming together" to face an emergency. Stress reactions save lives when, for instance, we dodge a falling object or run from the path of an oncoming vehicle. These physical reactions are caused by chemical changes in the brain.

What does happen to the body? Some of the same changes that occurred in Lod's frame also occur in Perry's body at the prospect of trying to muddle his way through the class presentation. They include increased heartbeat, labored breathing, sweaty palms, a tense feeling in the stomach, and difficulty in swallowing. What purposes do those changes serve?

Heavy breathing draws more oxygen into the lungs so we can keep going longer and faster. Rising blood pressure boosts the blood supply to the brain and muscles for greater and swifter activity. The digestive system shuts down, accounting for those knots and feathers in the stomach. Eye pupils dilate, allowing more light to enter and enabling us to see better. Extra adrenalin is pumped through the system for maximum activity. Blood-clotting mechanisms slow blood flow to prevent excessive bleeding from wounds. The production of *endorphins* (chemicals in the brain that alleviate pain) increases, which explains why a serious injury may not be felt at the time it occurs.

For Lod, these changes were appropriate. However, running from a wild beast or physically attacking an enemy requires a different kind of preparation from that needed for solving modern dilemmas. In today's world, stress often has to do with human relationships and adjusting to life in a constantly changing society. Many problems are not solved by avoidance or through physical encounters. Thus, instead of being helpful, stress reactions sometimes build up, causing emotional or physical discomfort, or both. For instance, *adrenalin*, that wonder hormone that can endow the body with superhuman strength, can also interfere with healing processes.

STRESS: WHAT'S GOOD ABOUT IT?

We may think of stress as something to be avoided. Yet life with no conflict would be dull and unstimulating. Dr.

Selye calls stress "the spice of life." Because of it, we are constantly adapting, changing to fit new circumstances. Stress can bring out our strengths. It can affect not just our physical strength, but also courage that we aren't aware of until we need it. What happens when a disaster such as flood or earthquake strikes a community? The first reaction of the people is survival, simply staying alive. When the tragedy subsides, the victims are in a state of shock. Within days, however, they are working to rebuild their community and their lives. They are discovering the marvels of teamwork. They are noting the differences between what is important in life and what is trivial. They are discovering the wonderful rewards of companionship. Stress is a necessary element in people-building and community-building.

We may think of stress as interfering with healthy development. Actually, it is essential to the growth of mature behavior. This was demonstrated in animal experiments conducted by psychologist Seymour Levine of Stanford University. Rats exposed to stress early in their lives developed normally and handled stress well later on. Rats not subjected to stress during infancy displayed timid, inadequate behavior as adults. The differences between the groups were not only behavioral, but chemical. The rats that had experienced stress in infancy had prompter, more effective reactions from the pituitary and adrenal glands. Apparently, human beings react to stress in similar ways.

STRESS: WHAT'S DANGEROUS ABOUT IT?

If stress is so remarkable, why does it contribute to the top killers, including coronary disease, accidental death, cancer, and suicide?

Stress is of two types—crises and day-to-day hassles. Thus, losing a home through fire can be a stressor, and so can attending a certain class. Ideally, we manage to handle the frustration of stress as it comes along. Our bodies and our emotions return to normal, either quickly or eventually. However, when we are bombarded with extremely traumatic experiences or when disturbances build up, we may not be able to heal and adjust normally. The result can be illness, depression, or anxiety.

Barbara B. Brown in *Between Health and Illness* emphasizes that the condition or incident that causes stress does not cause us to be sick. It is the emotional distress brought on by the stressor that triggers the illness. That is why it is important to deal with the causes of stress, rather than simply treating the resulting bodily symptoms.

According to Dr. Selye, when stress becomes chronic, long-term chemical changes occur in the body, such as high blood pressure or damage to organs. The body's immune system may break down, enabling viruses, bacteria, and infections to take over. Barbara Brown explains that the more we understand stress, the less tendency there is to react to future stress. As we learn to deal with stress in sensible and healthy ways, the regulating mechanisms of the body gradually allow a return to a normal or near-normal state.

HOW MUCH STRESS IS TOO MUCH?

Even for healthy families life is a parade of stressful situations. Constant change is going on, and that means that we continually have to make adjustments. A normal family will have crises that create unusual strain on its members. Stress is part of living, and most of the time we take it in stride.

For some persons and families, however, stress is continuous, a way of life. There is no opportunity for recovery.

Imagine what it would be like to live where there was not enough food to go around. All of your time and energy would be devoted to trying to find enough to eat to stay alive. Think of having no shelter, no place to think of as home—of being frozen in winter and scorched by a merciless sun in summer. What if you were a child in a country always at war. You may never have lived a single day of your life anywhere except on a battlefield. The closest thing to adventure or recreation might be shooting or throwing stones at the enemy.

Although conditions in our country are not that extreme, there are thousands of children who might be thought of as children of stress because their lives are a nightmare of substandard conditions over which they have little or no control. Sometimes this life-style is created by an individual through lack of effort, addiction to alcohol or other drugs, or getting caught up in a life of crime. But a baby does not choose to be born into a life of hopelessness.

COPING WITH STRESS

Stress is a result of a change or loss in a person's life. It is what happens when we'd rather it didn't. It is the uninvited intruder in the tranquility of our lives. There are three major reactions to an unpleasant stressful situation. (Remember, pleasant happenings can also cause stress.)

1. Distress—a feeling of not being able to cope.
2. Illness.
3. The galvanizing of energies to face and deal with adversity.

When under stress, we cry out for comfort. We want something to make our bodies and emotions feel better.

With a wealth of unprescribed chemicals at our fingertips, it is no wonder we are tempted to use some of them for instant relief. The most commonly used of these substances in our country is alcohol. It is legal (beyond a certain age), readily available, and socially approved by many people. It is also our number one drug problem from the standpoint of physical damage, monetary cost, and human suffering.

The teenager who reaches for alcohol or another drug during times of stress is adding more chemical alterations to a body already undergoing physical changes. The results can be disastrous.

NOT WORTH DYING FOR

Stress is a person's emotional reaction to an unusual or shocking event or circumstance. It produces both good and bad results. One of the adverse effects is illness. The most extreme price is death. Stress should not be allowed to reach the point at which the troubled person decides life is not worth living.

Do you know someone who might be considering suicide? How can you tell? Changes in personality or behavior may be clues.

You may be tempted not to deal with a deeply depressed or suicidal person for fear of saying or doing the wrong thing. It isn't so much a matter of the "right" or "wrong" thing, however, as it is an attitude of caring and being supportive.

Here is how teenager Hollis responded when her friend, Jill, began to take on a new personality. Hollis noticed that Jill wasn't fun to have around any more. She was frequently absent from school and seemed not to care that her grades were falling. There was no more laughing together, sharing of secrets, double dating, or going out for pizzas.

Where did my friend go? Hollis asked herself. Finally she decided to ask Jill. According to Hollis, their conversation went something like this:

Hollis: What's with you lately? You're not yourself anymore.

Jill: Who cares?

Hollis: I do, or I wouldn't be asking.

Jill: Well, if *you* do—which I doubt—you're the only one.

Hollis: Oh, come off it, Jill. What's really bugging you?

Jill: For starters, you knew Steve dumped me, didn't you?

Hollis: Well, yes, but that's not the end of the world. Teenagers get dumped all the time. We always think our romances are forever, but they hardly ever are.

Jill: I knew you wouldn't understand.

Hollis: Sure I understand. I've been dumped.

Jill: (showing a mild spark of interest) When?

Hollis: (giggling) In fifth grade by a boy named Gorell Moneypenny.

Jill: (not joining in the laughter) Big deal!

Hollis: It was a big deal then. Life is full of big deals. Later on they turn out to be little deals.

Jill: If there *is* a "later on."

Hollis: Does that mean you're thinking about bugging out?

Jill: You might say that.

Hollis remembers that those words sent a clutch of fear to her heart. She wished she hadn't suggested the idea of suicide, but there was no turning back now. She knew

there was no point in telling Jill what a beautiful world this is or how much we have to live for. Jill wouldn't have bought a word of it. Nor did Hollis mention that things would turn out okay. Jill wouldn't have believed that either. What she did say, was, "Well, I'll be hanging around close until we work through this crisis."

Jill: Promise you won't tell anyone about this, Hollis.

Hollis: Of course I won't make a promise like that. I'll tell counselors and anyone else I can think of who can help you feel better.

Jill: You wouldn't!

Hollis: You'd better believe I would. Would you stand at the lakeshore and watch someone drown?

Jill: I s'pose not.

Hollis: You'd *better* s'pose not. People don't just stand around and watch other people die needlessly.

Hollis did share Jill's confidence with the school counselor, who visited with Jill's parents. They in turn persuaded Jill to go with them to a mental health clinic for professional help for the entire family.

STRESS CAN'T CONTROL ME!

Sometimes we forget that life is not meant to be pain-free. It is a certainty that all of us are going to do some hurting, both physical and emotional. How do we avoid stress? Mostly we don't, and in fact we shouldn't. Our task is to recognize stress and face it, not attempt to run from it. In Hollis's words, "Life is full of big deals. Later on they turn out to be little deals."

CHAPTER ◇ 12

I Count, But
So Do You

The ancient Greeks fretted about the state of "modern society" and agonized over what the world was coming to. We are still wondering today what modern society is coming to. A famous writer moving from California to New York City reported that a third of the city was so dangerous that even the police wouldn't go there. That might sound quite up-to-date, but the report was written about one hundred years ago by Mark Twain.

Young people plead with their parent-generation to correct the turmoil, but down deep they know it is largely up to them.

Each generation journeys through adolescence somewhat differently from each other one, but with a quality of unity that distinguishes it, and with certain designations such as "flapper," "beatnik," "hipster," "hippie," "flower child," "yuppie," "freak," "baby boomer."

Toward the end of the 1980s a newspaper article carried the startling headline, "U.S. PRODUCING A LOST

GENERATION OF KIDS." The article, written by a police officer of twenty years, reported seeing for the first time "kids born without families, including a mother." Most of these, the officer predicted, are doomed almost with certainty to end up dead in the streets or alleys or spend most of their lives in jail.

By being born without a mother, the writer probably refers to those thousands of babies who will be abandoned by mothers, taken from mothers who are drug-addicted or otherwise unfit for parenthood, or born of mothers who die in childbirth, often due to neglect during pregnancy and delivery.

One thing we take for granted is the mother-child relationship. The possibility of that being erased at the time of birth places a huge question mark on the child's present and future well-being.

Are you willing to settle for going down i̇n history as the "lost generation"? Of course not. Not as long as most of you are doing an acceptable job of living. Not as long as you want a wonderful world for the children you may someday have.

THERE'S BAD NEWS OUT THERE

However good a job you are doing with your own life, a look around and attention to the media are reminders that our world is severely injured. Daily headlines scream the dismal news: 100,000 U.S. children homeless. Victim tells of danger of Satanic cults. Alcoholism America's number one drug problem. Society's love of sports leads many teens to steroid use. Study says urban children face bleak future. Three-way fight waged over surrogate child. Spread of teen cults has authorities worried. Denver police note rise in racist "skinhead" gang activity. Fetal alcohol syndrome becoming a serious problem. Study finds "latchkey kids" more likely to become substance abusers. Five-year-old turns parents in to police for cocaine use. Ten million U.S. children come from broken homes. Female street gangs form in Chicago.

DO WE HOLD STILL FOR THAT?

In spite of all the gloomy news, society is not dying. Too many individuals and groups are out there who won't let that happen. Here's a sampling of "hope" headlines: Tough Love provides parental support. The "Adam Project" helps those who physically abuse others. Teens look at America in book by students. Abused kids may not grow up to be abusive parents. Teens urge passage of grant program for school clinics. Good schools for poor children. Teens can prevent suicides. Think of Crisis Helpline as part of your family. Underprivileged sixth-graders earn money to give to others. Operation Brightside: Inner-city teens working to help senior citizens. Walt Clark students study world hunger. Willow Place: An address for working toward self-sufficiency. Project Challenge gives youth brighter vision for the future. Survey shows adult awareness of teen problems is growing.

The list of people helping people goes on indefinitely. No matter what your problem, help is available in practically any community. Notice how many of the foregoing headlines involve teenagers and children. The most encouraging thing about today is that the affairs of society don't belong just to adults or to separate groups. Communities are coming together as never before to include parents, schools, law enforcement personnel, church groups, youth groups, medical and mental health and social service workers, adolescents and children.

YOU CAN'T CHANGE THE WORLD ALL BY YOURSELF

There isn't much you can do by yourself to change the statistics about social issues. However, the way you live your life, the changes that take place in you, can have immense impact on your own well-being and on the people in your life. The effects can be destructive or constructive, depending on how you feel about yourself and others. Basically, there are only four philosophies in dealing with people: I count; you don't. You count; I don't. I don't count, and neither do you. We both count.

Let's see how these work.

1. *I count; you don't*. Crystal didn't like the rules at home and at school, so she ran away. She didn't let her family know where she was.
2. *You count; I don't*. Twenty-six-year-old Gertrude gave up marriage to stay home with her widowed mother.
3. *I don't count; and neither do you*. Rowland is addicted to crack cocaine. He has given up his job and dropped out of school. He expects his parents to support him and his habit.
4. *We both count*. High-school graduate Gail C. has been accepted at the university of her choice in another state. The week before she is to go, her father has a heart attack. Although he recovers, he is to be bedridden for a time and will be under strict medical care for several months. Gail decides she should stay at home to help with her father's care and get a job to help with medical expenses. Her parents insist that she should not make that sacrifice. They don't want her to stay out of school

for a year, making it harder to pick up her education later. The family finally decides on a compromise. Gail will attend the two-year community college in her hometown for a year, working part-time, and then go away to school the following year. The solution is arrived at because each member of the family is convinced that everyone's needs count.

CHAPTER 13

Being Me While
Satisfying You

Twenty-five-year-old Tim remarked to his father, "Dad, I get more like you every day."

The father's response was, "It's too bad you weren't more like me when you were a teenager."

Both men laughed, knowing that it wasn't "too bad" at all. They are aware that being a typical teenager is training ground for adulthood, and typical teenagers aren't just like their parents. Even so, each generation would like to see some changes in the other.

I WISH . . .

Standard complaints expressed by most parents include wishing that their kids would: Pay attention to what we parents tell them. Talk to us. Get better grades. Take school seriously. Not monopolize the telephone. Obey family rules. Come in on time. Not argue with everything we say. Not hang around with a certain crowd. Be less obvious about sex and other intimate matters. Clean up their language. Not act as if they know everything. Dress decently. Think seriously about the future. Quit blaming our generation for "trashing" the world.

Adolescents' wishes about their parents often include the following: Stay out of my affairs. Like my friends. Think like me. Come to athletic events (and other performances) I am involved in. Let me have a car. Let me drive the family car. Understand me. Practice the same things they expect of me, like being honest and not smoking and drinking. Trust me. Talk to me. Listen to me. Keep their promises. Quit worrying so much about what people will think. Quit hounding me about grades. Quit nagging me about the future. Allow me to take some risks. Quit fighting.

Things young people wish their parents would not do include: Get a divorce. Criticize the way I dress. Embarrass me in front of my friends. Be so protective of me. Hate each other.

Sound familiar? You can no doubt add to each list. Many of these complaints are fairly constant from generation to generation. Several have to do with age differences; they won't change appreciably. Some are deserving of careful attention because they have to do with the quality of the family's health and stability.

TOWARD A HEALTHY FAMILY

Both generations mention the desire for more communication—talking and being listened to. No matter how far apart you and your parents are in belief and behavior, you are alike in feelings. Talking about those emotions can bring families closer together if the members are careful about *how* they express themselves.

Trust is one of the constants in human relationships. You wish your parents would trust you. Your part in that is to prove that they can. You want them to keep their promises. You want them to be someone you can count on, and they want the same of you.

You think your parents should be good examples by observing the same expectations they have of you. This is one of the most important rules to keep in mind if you someday become a parent. Parents are teachers. Children learn how to be parents from living with parents.

WHAT WILL THE NEIGHBORS SAY!

A common annoyance of young people throughout the ages is parents' emphasis on the family image. Junior-high student Delphie comments on that: "You know how parents are forever worrying for fear their kids will get their names in the paper for doing something bad? So imagine how I felt when a kid at school said, 'I see where your old man got picked up for drunk driving.' I didn't know what to say, so I laughed and pretended I thought it was funny. All I wanted was for the floor to open."

Teenager Dominick also has an opinion about "what people will think." He says, "It's always been parents harping about what people are saying about the family. Always worrying about the kids doing something to disgrace them. Nowadays it's us kids who do a lot of the squirming. For instance, what do you say when people ask you about your father, and as far as you know you never had a father. Of course you could say, 'The old boy skipped out before I was born.' Instead you make up some kind of a lie."

WHAT DO YOU TELL PEOPLE?

When people get acquainted, the conversation usually comes around to family. Most of us have some embarrassing things about our family that we would just as soon not talk about. For many teenagers, it is awkward or impossible to discuss issues like divorce (especially if one of your parents has had several divorces), single parents, homosexual parents, stepparents, alcoholic relatives, abusive or incestuous parents, parents' live-ins, runaway parents, family members in prison, and other intimate situations. It is your right to explain what you feel like talking about, being as honest as possible without letting people wade around in your private life. Learn to say, "That's something I don't want to talk about." There may be some secrets you cannot share with anyone.

INDIVIDUALITY VERSUS CONFORMITY

A perplexing aspect of expectations is trying to live up to them and at the same time be an individual. Nonconforming behavior represents conflict between self and society, often leading to trouble.

How can we accept the contradiction of being ourselves and being one of "the crowd"? Let's observe a student experiencing this problem. After Psychology class one day, Dane complained to his teacher that his classmates ridiculed him for dressing strangely.

Mr. Gorski said, "You'll have to admit that the sailor middy blouse, the pointed-toe high shoes, and that rope of padlocks around your head are attention-getters."

"Hey, man, most everybody dresses nutty nowadays."

Mr. Gorski nodded. "True, but there's nutty and there's nuttier."

"But you haven't answered my question. Do people have the right to make fun of me?" Dane demanded.

"You have a right to dress the way you want to, and people have the right to react as they want to. The question isn't *should* your peers accept you in that garb; it's *do* they accept you?"

"So in other words, I have to be like other people to be accepted," Dane challenged.

Mr. Gorski said, "To a degree, Let's talk about it in class tomorrow."

After the class discussion about individuality and conformity, Mr. Gorski gave a homework assignment. "During the week, observe a group performing a regular routine. The participants are to be dressed alike and going through motions in unison. They can be cheerleaders, dancers, choral singers, a military drill team. They can be on TV or in person. Your assignment is to observe these performers both as a group and as individuals. Determine how they are alike and how they differ."

After completing their observations, the students offered the following comments: "One of the dancers was smoother in his movements than the others." "One cheerleader acted as if she thought she was pretty hot stuff." "The drill team members were all different sizes and shapes. Some had jerky movements, some smooth." "Some of the singers acted really animated as if they were having a good time, while some of them barely opened their mouth or changed expression."

Mr. Gorski said, "Good observations. The point of the assignment is that we are individuals even when we are conforming. Our unique personalities save us from drowning. When you are expected to go along with the crowd, you might do it a little differently."

FEELING TRAPPED?

Being an individual within the group is what life amounts to, but most of us rebel at times against the demands of our family and our world. A feeling of being trapped was expressed by one of Mr. Gorski's students, who wrote, "I get caught up in my machine-like days. Are they teaching me, or are they conditioning me so I won't think for myself?"

A second student expressed the need to belong, to be like others: "Sometimes I feel as if all the rest of the people were made from the same cookie cutter. They are all perfect. Then someone took the leftover scraps and made me."

I DON'T CARE WHAT PEOPLE THINK. OR DO I?

We often get tired of trying to please others. "I don't care what people think of me," you say. However, what others think of you determines how they treat you. The way you are treated, in turn, has much to with how you feel about yourself. That is as true within your family as it is in the rest of your world. How you feel about yourself is reflected in behavior—desirable and undesirable. Each segment of the cycle triggers another segment. If you want to change another person's behavior toward you, you must work on the segment of the cycle that you can control—your own actions and attitudes. Care about yourself and care about those other people. Accept yourself and accept them for what they are. George Calden, author of *I Count—You Count*, wrote, "The greatest You-Count attitude I can show you is to accept you as you are."

WALKING AWAY FROM CHILDHOOD?

Meantime, your overwhelming task is to become grown-up. The psychologists speak of the major task of adolescence as "self-actualization." Stated simply, that means becoming what we are desirous and capable of becoming. Steps toward that process begin during infancy when the child tries out various roles. The ones adopted are those that bring rewarding responses. From which role might a baby get the most favorable attention—spoiled darling, little showoff, whiner, pouter? Or does he or she finally discover that just being a nice kid to have around works best?

All through our lives, the behaviors that are rewarded and encouraged are the ones that become part of our personality.

Your present task in achieving self-actualization is learning to be on your own. Certainly no one is ever totally independent. We rely on one another for jobs, medical services, food, public utilities, education and protection, to name a few of our dependencies. However we achieve tremendous independence when we are able to manage our own lives within the confines of society. That means having freedom and at the same time recognizing the limits within which we must operate. The poet Robert Frost described freedom as "moving easy in harness."

"Leaving home" is not simply the physical process of moving out of the family household. It is a psychological separation as well. Nineteen-year-old Rolly moved out because his father told him to "shape up or ship out." By "shaping up," his father had in mind to get off drugs, find a job, and obey family rules. Rolly decided to move out. He now drifts from job to job, living mainly off welfare. He has shifted his dependency from parents to taxpayers.

Most of us leave our childhood homes. The concern is not so much when we leave as why and how. Leaving home need not mean forsaking the primary family. Nor does getting out on our own mean we have reached self-actualization. It is only one giant step in the process.

LOVINGLY YOURS

Which is more painful—outgrowing parenthood or outgrowing childhood? Both, depending on which you are, parent or youth.

The following is an except from a letter a parent wrote to her married daughter:

"If I could only start being a parent all over again! Correct all those mistakes I made. Erase a lot of the things I said. Put into practice the wisdom I have acquired. Work harder at earning your love and respect. I concentrated so hard on trying to give you my beliefs and values that I sometimes closed my ears to yours. Because I know youth must learn from age, I worked too hard at protecting you from your own mistakes. I was so preoccupied with the child I was creating for the world that I sometimes lost sight of those invisible scratches and bruises on the inside where your feelings are."

As part of his final exam for Adolescent Psychology class, Clay Porter wrote about kids growing away from their parents:

"I know I have been giving my parents (and teachers) a bad time lately. It's kind of hard to say why. I guess it has something to do with moods. Part of the time

I'm angry without knowing why. The next day I'm feeling great again. A human yo-yo, that's me. It's almost as if I don't know me. I keep asking myself, 'Now why did I say that!' or 'Why can't I tell people how I really feel?' It's because I don't know how to grow away from home that I talk big and bully my way along. My voice says one thing and my body does something else.

"Our psychology teacher says we're a real puzzle at this age because we're secretly scared of growing up, but at the same time we're scared our parents won't let us. I think part of my trouble is knowing that my parents are right most of the time but not wanting to admit it. If I go along with what they say, it's the same as saying I'm still a little kid who can't think for myself. If I make my own decisions, it's my way of telling everyone (including myself) that I'm able to manage on my own. (I wish I really believed that!) I want to tell grown-ups that I have to go it on my own, even when my decisions aren't wise ones. I still need their help and support, though, even when I reject it. What I'd really like to tell my parents is that I think they're great (even my stepmother) and that I love them. It's just that the words don't come out that way. I hear myself saying something else, like, 'When are you ever going to let me grow up?' Why is it so hard to say, 'I love you'?"

EVERYONE NEEDS A PARENT

Thousands of children are born into a world of hopelessness and have a rocky time from then on. If they have parenting, it is a kind that doesn't count for much. Some have never known a home or a true family. You may be one of those. Most of you others probably began life under at least reasonably stable conditions. Where do you go from here? The advice to all of you is the same. *Learn to be a good parent to yourself.* In the long run, everyone is his or her own parent.

Having too little woe in life can be a handicap. The more adversities you have encountered, the more problem-solving skills you may have acquired. No matter what your past has been, the future is yours to shape.

Ideally, every child should have two wise and loving parents. Close to half of children will spend at least part of their childhood and youth in single-parent homes. Some will not have even one adequate parent. Are they doomed? In a study of military families, it was concluded that emotionally healthy mothers are able to counteract the effects of the father's absence. We must not assume that children must grow up with two parents in order to be psychologically and physically healthy.

It is possible to have parenting without having a parent. Even parents need parenting sometimes. For instance, suppose you come home from school and find your mother dragging around with the flu. You may be the logical "parent" in this instance, so you say, "You go on to bed, Mom. I'll get supper."

MY EXPECTATIONS FOR ME

But about being a parent to yourself—how do you do that? You act like a parent, which means that you measure what you do by the criterion, "Is this good for me?" Your answer will have to be "no" to any form of runningawayness— chemical crutches (including alcohol and other nonprescribed drugs), leaving home with nowhere to go, dropping out of school, street gang involvement, becoming dependent on society, criminal activity, reckless driving, and other unnecessary risks. If you are a good parent, you will forbid activity that endangers your life, your health, or your future.

HELP!

The problem is, if you are feeling hopeless, helpless, and out of control your main concern won't be to act like a wise parent. You will be seeking some way to blot out the pain. That's when you cry "Help!"

If you broke a leg, you probably wouldn't try to set it. If your life is broken, don't try to fix it by yourself. Now is the time to experience the bonding that you may have missed out on at birth. Somewhere out there in that ash-colored world are people who care what happens to you. Allow them to love you and to help you. Who are they?

They are too many to list, but practically every community has social services, mental health services, hotlines, safe facilities for abused families, Alcoholics Anonymous, Al-Anon and Alateen for families with alcohol problems, drug-abuse clinics, Tough Love for parents of problem young adults, Big Brothers and Big Sisters, and dozens more. Most communities are establishing training programs to teach work skills as part of their rehabilitation efforts. For example, Denver's Operation Brightside is a program that employs inner-city teens to work at senior citizen centers doing repairing, painting, and other needed improvements. What could do more for self-esteem than being paid to help others?

How do you find one of these opportunities to be the worthwhile person each of us was meant to be? First of all, choose someone you admire and feel you can trust. This may be a school counselor, a rabbi or minister, a teacher, the parent of one of your friends, your doctor, or anyone else you can establish a bond with. Or use the yellow pages of your phone directory for advice about professional services that you can afford. Hotlines and helplines are not only for listening to your problems; they furnish information about other sources you can turn to.

Even healthy families need support groups and other kinds of comfort and aid from time to time. Asking for help is not a sign of weakness; it is a measure of wisdom.

WHAT ABOUT YOUR "SOMEDAY" FAMILY?

Miss Alvarez's class has concluded that although we certainly need to learn methods of parenting, there are many different ways of being adequate parents. Certainly the families of the pupils in that one class had many different philosophies and parenting practices.

"And just look how great we all turned out!" Perry said.

Miss Alvarez said, "Perry, we laughed when you said that, but it happens to be true. Here we are, a roomful of normal people, with many of the same beliefs and goals in spite of our differing backgrounds. Now as you go your separate ways, remember that you hold the world in your hands. Don't drop it. It already needs a lot of mending."

Suggested Reading

NONFICTION:

Berman, Claire. *What Am I Doing in a Stepfamily?* Secaucus, NJ: Lyle Stuart, Inc., 1982.

Boeckman, Charles. *Surviving Your Parents' Divorce.* New York: Franklin Watts, Inc., 1980.

Buckalew, M.W., Jr. *Learning to Control Stress.* New York: Richards Rosen Press, 1982.

Buscaglia, Leo F. *Living, Loving and Learning.* New York: Ballantine Books, 1982.

Calden, George. *I Count—You Count.* Niles, IL: Argus Communications, 1976.

Carlson, Dale. *Where's Your Head? Psychology for Teenagers.* New York: Atheneum, 1977.

Curran, Dolores. *Stress and the Healthy Family.* San Francisco: Harper & Row, Publisher, 1987.

Ginott, Haim G. *Between Parent and Teenager.* New York: Avon Books, 1971.

Krementz, Jill. *How It Feels to Be Adopted.* New York: Alfred Knopf, 1988.

———. *How It Feels When a Parent Dies.* New York: Alfred Knopf, 1981.

———. *How It Feels When Parents Divorce.* New York: Alfred Knopf, 1988.

Madaras, Lynda. *Lynda Madaras Talks to Teens About AIDS.* New York: Newmarket Press, 1988.

Rofes, Eric, ed. *The Kids' Book of Divorce—By, For & About Kids.* Lexington, MA: The Lewis Publishing Company, Inc., 1981.

FICTION:

Blume, Judy. *Tiger Eyes*. New York: Bradbury Press, 1981. (loss)

Colman, Hila. *Nobody Told Me What I Need to Know*. New York: William Morrow and Co., 1984. (in search of self; protective family)

———. *The Family Trap*. New York: William Morrow and Co., 1982.

Klein, Norma. *Confessions of an Only Child*. New York: Pantheon, 1974.

Lowry, Lois. *Switcharound*. Boston: Houghton Mifflin, 1985. (divorce)

Mazer, Norma Fox. *Someone to Love*. New York: Delacorte, 1984. (teen live-ins)

———. *Silver*. New York: Morrow Junior Books, 1988. (single-parent, low-income family; incest)

Okimoto Jean Davies. *It's Just Too Much*. New York: G.P. Putnam's Sons, 1980. (remarriage)

Pfeffer, Susan Beth. *Just Morgan*. New York: Henry Z. Walck, 1970. (orphan)

———. *The Year Without Michael*. New York: Bantam, 1987. (family member missing)

Rodowsky, Colby. *Julie's Daughter*. New York: Farrar, Straus and Giroux, 1985. (daughter deserted by mother)

Veglahn, Nancy. *Fellowship of the Seven Stars*. Nashville, TN: Abingdon Press, 1981. (cult involvement)

YOUNG ADULT NOVELS WITH SPECIAL INTEREST FOR BOYS (AS WELL AS FOR GIRLS)

Cone, Molly. *Paul David Silverman Is a Father*. New York: E.P. Dutton, 1983. (teen parenthood)

Cormier, Robert. *I Am the Cheese*. New York: Pantheon, 1977. (unlocking the past)

————. *The Bumblebee Flies Away*. New York: Pantheon, 1983. (death; terminal care facility)

————. *The Chocolate War*. New York: Pantheon, 1974. (individuality vs. conformity)

Gauch, Patricia. *Morelli's Game*. New York: G.P. Putnam's Sons, 1981. (individual vs. team)

Greene, Sheppard. *The Boy Who Drank Too Much*. New York: Viking, 1979. (teen alcoholism)

Guy, Rosa. *The Disappearance*. New York: Delacorte, 1979. (racial discrimination)

Henthoff, Nat. *The Day They Came to Arrest the Book*. New York: Delacorte, 1982. (individual rights vs. censorship)

Hinton, E.S. *Taming the Star Runner*. New York: Delacorte, 1988. (sibling problem)

————. *The Outsiders*. New York: Dell, 1967. (need to belong)

Mazer, Harry. *Hey, Kid! Does She Love Me?* New York: Thomas Y. Crowell, 1984. (teen parenthood)

————. *When the Phone Rang*. New York: Thomas Y. Crowell, 1985. (death of parents)

Peck, Richard. *Father Figure*. New York: Viking, 1978. (father-son turmoil)

Phipson, Joan. *Hit and Run*. New York: Atheneum, 1985. (teen delinquency; finding self)

Roos, Stephen. *You'll Miss Me When I'm Gone*. New York: Delacorte, 1988. (teen alcoholism)

Index